How To Reduce Landlord Taxes

Tax Saving Tips To Help Boost Your Property Profits!

By

Arthur Weller & Amer Siddiq

Publisher Details
This guide is published by Tax Portal Ltd. 3 Sanderson Close, Great Sankey, Warrington, Cheshire, WA5 3LN.

'How to Reduce Landlord Taxes' – First published in May 2009. Second Edition April 2010. Third Edition July 2010. Fourth Edition April 2011. Fifth Edition April 2012. Sixth Edition April 2013. Seventh edition May 2014. Eighth edition April 2015. Ninth Edition April 2016. Tenth Edition April 2017. Eleventh Edition April 2018. Twelfth Edition March 2019. Thirteenth Edition May 2020.

Copyright
The right of Arthur Weller and Tax Portal Ltd to be identified as the authors of this guide has been asserted in accordance with the Copyright, Designs and Patents Act 1988, England.

© 2009-2020 Arthur Weller and Tax Portal Ltd

A CIP Copy of this book is available from the British Library.

978-1-9996405-8-3

Trademarks
Property Tax Portal, Tax Portal Ltd and other Tax Portal Ltd services/ products referenced in this guide are registered trademarks or trademarks of Tax Portal Ltd in the UK and/or other countries.

Disclaimer

1. This guide is produced for General guidance only, and professional advice should be sought before any decision is made. Individual circumstances can vary and therefore no responsibility can be accepted by the author, Arthur Weller, or the publisher Tax Portal Ltd, for any action taken, or any decision made to refrain from action, by any readers of this guide.

2. Tax rules and legislation are constantly changing and therefore the information printed in this guide is correct at the time of printing – April 2020.

3. Neither the author nor Tax Portal Ltd offer financial, legal or investment advice. If you require such advice then, we urge you to seek the opinion of an appropriate professional in the relevant field. We care about your success and therefore encourage you to take appropriate advice before you put any of your financial or other resources at risk. Don't forget, investment values can decrease as well as increase.

4. To the fullest extent permitted by law, Arthur Weller and Tax Portal Ltd do not accept liability for any direct, indirect, special, consequential or other losses or damages of whatsoever kind arising from using this guide.

   The guide itself is provided 'as is' without express or implied warranty.

5. Arthur Weller and Tax Portal Ltd reserve the right to alter any part of this guide at any time without notice

Contents

1. **About The Authors** **15**

   1.1. **Arthur Weller - The Property Tax Specialist** _____ 15

   1.2. **Amer Siddiq - The Landlord** _____ 15

   1.3. **Acknowledgements** _____ 16

2. **The Importance Of Tax Planning** **17**

   2.1. **Knowing When To Consider Planning** _____ 17

      2.1.1. Buying...17
      2.1.2. Repairs And Refurbishment 18
      2.1.3. Selling 18
      2.1.4. Life Changes 19
      2.1.5. Politics 19
      2.1.6. End And Start Of The Tax Year 19

   2.2. **The Real Benefits Of Tax Planning** _____ 20

      2.2.1. Paying Less Tax 20
      2.2.2. Clear 'Entrance' And 'Exit' Strategies 20
      2.2.3. Staying Focused..20
      2.2.4. Improving Cash Flow 21
      2.2.5. Avoiding Common Tax Traps 21

   2.3. **Asking HMRC For Tax Advice** _____ 21

      2.3.1. Making Use Of HMRC Services 21
      2.3.2. The Drawback 22
      2.3.3. Practical Tip 22

3. **Making Tax Digital For Landlords** **23**

   3.1. **What Is Making Tax Digital?** _____ 23

   3.2. **What Has Changed?** _____ 23

   3.3. **Submission Dates** _____ 24

      3.3.1. Real Time Basis...24

   3.4. **When Is MTD Starting?** _____ 24

      3.4.1. Stage 1 24
      3.4.2. Stages 2 And 3..25

   3.5. **Which Landlords Will Be Affected?** _____ 25

   3.6. **MTD Compliance** _____ 25

      3.6.1. All Landlords..25
      3.6.2. Multiple Properties 26
      3.6.3. Jointly Owned Properties 26
      3.6.4. How And When Will Tax Payments Be Made?....................26

3.7.   The New System Of Penalties _____ 26

3.8.   Current Penalty System _____ 27

    3.8.1.   VAT Registered Furnished Holiday Lets 27
    3.8.2.   Other Landlords...27

3.9.   Simplified 'Cash Basis' For Unincorporated Property Businesses _____ 27

3.10.   Current Situation _____ 27

3.11.   Possible Timetable For 2021/22 _____ 27

3.12.   Final Points _____ 28

3.13.   Invest In Landlord Software _____ 28

4.   *Understanding Your Tax Liabilities* 29

5.   *Income Tax Liabilities For Investors/Traders* 32

5.1.   Property Investor _____ 32

5.2.   Property Traders/Dealers_____ 32

5.3.   Income Tax Rates _____ 32

5.4.   Income Tax Calculation Case Studies_____ 33

    5.4.1.   Income Tax Calculation For Property Investors...33
    5.4.2.   Income Tax Calculation For Property Developers..35

6.   *Owning Properties As A Sole Trader* 37

6.1.   Buying Properties As A Sole Trader _____ 37

6.2.   When Is It Tax Efficient To Buy Property As A Sole Trader?_____ 37

6.3.   When Is It NOT Tax Efficient To Buy Property As A Sole Trader? _____ 38

6.4.   A Note About Selling Properties When Operating As A Sole Trader _____ 39

7.   *Income Tax & Property Partnerships* 40

7.1.   What Is A Property Partnership? _____ 40

    7.1.1.   Joint Tenants 40
    7.1.2.   Tenants In Common...40

7.2.   When To Consider Buying In A Partnership_____ 41

7.3.   Partners Must Be TRUSTWORTHY _____ 41

7.4.   Partnerships Between Husband And Wife_____ 42

7.5.   Partnerships Between Those Other Than A Husband And Wife_____ 43

7.6.   How To Declare A Partnership Split to HMRC_____ 43

7.7.   Moving Properties Into Joint Ownership To Avoid Income Tax_____ 44

    7.7.1.   Three Simple Steps To Follow 44
    7.7.2.   Typical Costs Incurred When Transferring 45

8.   *How To Jointly Own A Property 50:50 But Split Rental Income 90:10!* 47

  8.1.   What Has To Be Done? _____ 47

  8.2.   How Does This Work In Practice? _____ 47

  8.3.   What Does HMRC Think Of This Arrangement? _____ 48

  8.4.   Property Owners Who Are Married Couples _____ 48

  8.5.   Getting It Right! _____ 48

9.   *Joint Property And Form 17: Practical Points* 50

  9.1.   Splitting Income Differently _____ 50

  9.2.   Points To Watch _____ 50

    9.2.1.   Practical Tip 51

10. *Legal v Beneficial Ownership: A 'Taxing' Distinction!* 52

  10.1. Legal And Beneficial Ownership _____ 52

  10.2. Legal Ownership _____ 52

  10.3. Beneficial Ownership _____ 52

  10.4. Analogies _____ 53

  10.5. Tax Implications _____ 53

  10.6. Tax Complications _____ 54

    10.6.1.   Income Tax 54
    10.6.2.   Capital Gains Tax 54
    10.6.3.   Inheritance Tax 54
    10.6.4.   Practical Tip 54

11. *Offsetting Interest Charges From 6ᵗʰ April 2017* 55

  11.1. Restricting Tax Relief On Mortgage Interest And Related Finance Costs __ 55

    11.1.1.   Will It Affect Me? 55
    11.1.2.   Partnerships, Companies And Trusts 56
    11.1.3.   How Will It Affect Me? 56
    11.1.4.   When Will It Affect Me? 57
    11.1.5.   Examples Of New Interest Relief Tax Rules 57
    11.1.6.   What Should I Do? 58

12. *Offsetting Different Types Of Interest Charges* 60

  12.1. Interest On Mortgages _____ 60

  12.2. A Note About 'Interest Only' And 'Repayment Mortgages' _____ 61

    12.2.1.   Interest Only Mortgage 61
    12.2.2.   Repayment Mortgage 61

12.3.   **Interest On Personal Loans** _____ 62

    12.3.1.   Loan Used For Providing Deposit..62
    12.3.2.   Loan Used For Refurbishments/Developments...........................63
    12.3.3.   Loans Used For Purchasing Products.......................................64
    12.3.4.   Loans To Continue The Running Of Your Business.....................64
    12.3.5.   Interest On Overdrafts...65

12.4.   **Interest On Re-Mortgages** _____ 65

13.   *'Wholly And Exclusively'*.. 68

13.1.   **Understanding The Term 'Wholly And Exclusively'** _____ 68

13.2.   **What If Cost Is Not Wholly And Exclusively Incurred For Property?** _____ 68

13.3.   **Costs Of Maintenance And Repairs** _____ 69

13.4.   **Typical Maintenance/Repair Costs** _____ 70

13.5.   **The Big Misconception About Costs When A Property Is First Let?** _____ 70

    13.5.1.   Allowable Expenses 70
    13.5.2.   The Test...71
    13.5.3.   A Cinema..71
    13.5.4.   A Ship...71
    13.5.5.   Is Your Property A Cinema Or A Ship?..................................71

13.6.   **Capital Improvements** _____ 72

14.   *Replacing Your Fixtures And Fittings*.................................. 73

14.1.   **What Are Fixtures And Fittings?** _____ 73

14.2.   **Replacing Fixtures And Fittings** _____ 73

    14.2.1.   Like-For-Like Replacement...74
    14.2.2.   What If It Is Not Possible To Replace With Like-For-Like? 74
    14.2.3.   Like-For-Like Replacement But With Capital Improvements........75
    14.2.4.   Replacement With Superior Fixture And Fittings......................75

15.   *Other Ways To Reduce Your Income Tax Bill*........................ 76

15.1.   **Rents, Rates, And Insurance** _____ 76

    15.1.1.   Rents..76
    15.1.2.   Rates..76
    15.1.3.   Insurance 76

15.2.   **Can I Offset Pre-Trading Expenditure?** _____ 77

15.3.   **Carrying Over Rental Losses** _____ 77

15.4.   **Claiming Travel Costs** _____ 78

    15.4.1.   *'Wholly And Exclusively'*...78
    15.4.2.   Office Based At Home 78
    15.4.3.   Office Outside Of Home...79
    15.4.4.   Use Of A Letting Agent..79
    15.4.5.   Relevant Tax Cases 79
    15.4.6.   How Much To Claim?..79

15.4.7.	Misc. Travel Costs	80
15.4.8.	Foreign Travel	80
15.4.9.	Expenses When Not Available For Letting	80

15.5.   General Property Costs **80**

15.6.   Storage Costs **81**

15.7.   Other Common Landlord Expenditures **81**

15.8.   Can I Offset The Cost Of A Property Seminar? **82**

15.9.   Capital Allowances For Landlords **83**

16.   *Running Your Property Business From Home* **84**

16.1.   Nature Of Relief **84**

16.2.   Typical Fixed Costs **84**

16.3.   Insurance **84**

16.4.   Council Tax **85**

16.5.   Mortgage Costs **85**

16.6.   Rent **85**

16.7.   Repairs And Maintenance **85**

16.7.1.	Practical Tip	86

17.   *Tenant Deposits: Traps & Tips* **87**

17.1.   Deposits From Tenants **87**

17.2.   Security Deposits **87**

17.3.   Holding Deposit **88**

17.3.1.	Practical Tip	89

17.4.   Tax Treatment Of 'Gifted Deposits'? **89**

17.4.1.	Gifted Deposit Schemes	89
17.4.2.	Tax Treatment	90
17.4.3.	Practical Tip	90

18.   *Cash Basis v Accruals Basis* **91**

18.1.   Cash Basis For Traders **92**

18.2.   Legislation And Guidance **92**

18.3.   Extension Of Cash Basis To Unincorporated Property Businesses **93**

18.4.   Cash Basis By Default **93**

18.5.   Eligibility – The Cash Basis Tests **94**

18.6.   Opting For The Accruals Basis _____ 97

18.7.   Multiple Property Businesses _____ 97

18.8.   Joint Owners _____ 98

18.9.   Joint Owners – Married Couples And Civil Partners _____ 99

18.10.   Calculation Of Property Business Profits On The Cash Basis ___ 100

18.11.   Income _____ 100

18.12.   Expenditure _____ 101

18.13.   No Accruals And Prepayments Or Debtors Or Creditor _____ 101

18.14.   Lease Premiums _____ 102

18.15.   Security Deposits _____ 102

18.16.   Capital Expenditure _____ 102

18.17.   Replacement Of Domestic Items _____ 103

18.18.   Capital Allowances – Cars _____ 104

18.19.   Mileage Rates _____ 104

18.20.   Relief For Interest _____ 104

18.21.   VAT _____ 105

18.22.   Entering The Cash Basis _____ 105

18.23.   Leaving The Cash Basis _____ 105

18.24.   Planning And Timing Issues _____ 106

18.25.   Final Thoughts _____ 106

19.   *Can A Limited Company Improve YOUR Tax Position?* *107*

19.1.   The Most Commonly Asked Tax Questions _____ 107

19.2.   Transferring Properties Into A Limited Company _____ 107

19.3.   Don't Forget Stamp Duty! _____ 108

19.4.   Understanding 'Limited Liability' _____ 108

19.5.   Two Major Tax Benefits Of Using A Limited Company _____ 110

19.6.   Other Benefits/Drawbacks Of A Limited Company _____ 110

19.6.1.   Benefits 110
19.6.2.   Drawbacks 111

20. Does Incorporation Stack Up For Landlords?..112

   20.1.   **Why Should I Incorporate?** _____ 112

   20.2.   **Why Is Incorporation Relief Useful?** _____ 114

   20.3.   **Incorporation Relief Route** _____ 115

   20.4.   **Mechanics – Transferring Liabilities** _____ 115

   20.5.   **Paying CGT By Instalments** _____ 117

       20.5.1.   Instalment Options – Requirements 117
       20.5.2.   Instalment Options – Mechanism 117
       20.5.3.   Other Considerations 119
       20.5.4.   Paying By Instalments Conclusion 119

21. Will A Property Management Company Save Me Tax?...................120

   21.1.   **Draw Up Formal Contracts Between You and Your Company** _____ 121

   21.2.   **Beware Of Artificial Transactions!** _____ 121

22. Saving On Stamp Duty..122

   22.1.   **When Do Property Investors Pay Stamp Duty?** _____ 122

       22.1.1.   Stamp Duty When Buying New Land Or Property 122
       22.1.2.   Stamp Duty When Transferring A Property 123

23. Tax-Free Income For Renting Out Part Of Your Home...................125

   23.1.   **What Is The Rent-A-Room Relief?** _____ 125

   23.2.   **Choosing Not to Use The Relief** _____ 126

   23.3.   **Renting Out In Joint Ownership** _____ 127

24. Generous Tax Breaks For Holiday Lets 128

   24.1.   **Qualifying Criteria For A Holiday Let** _____ 128

   24.2.   **Three Generous Tax Benefits Associated With Holiday Lets** _____ 128

       24.2.1.   Offsetting losses against other income 129
       24.2.2.   Re-investment Of Capital Gains 129
       24.2.3.   FHL – New Rules 129

25. Tax Implications When Converting Properties Into Flats 131

   25.1.   **Scenario 1** _____ 131

   25.2.   **Scenario 2** _____ 131

   25.3.   **Scenario 3** _____ 132

   25.4.   **Scenario 4** _____ 133

26. Understanding Capital Gains Tax (CGT) 135

   26.1.   **When You Are Liable to Pay CGT** _____ 135

26.2.   Recent History And Changes To The CGT Rate _____ 136

26.3.   How Your CGT Bill Is Calculated _____ 136

28.   *Reporting And Tax Payment Changes From 6ᵗʰ April 2020* 139

28.1.   When May A Residential Property Gain Arise? _____ 139

28.2.   Higher Tax Rates For Residential Property Gains _____ 139

28.3.   Reporting Pre-6 April 2020 Residential Property Gains_____ 139

28.4.   New Rules From 6 April 2020 _____ 140

28.5.   Requirement To Make A Payment On Account _____ 140

28.6.   Calculating The Payment On Account _____ 140

28.7.   Finalising The Position _____ 141

29.   *Private Residence Relief (PPR)* 142

29.1.   What Is Private Residence Relief?_____ 142

29.1.1.   Full Residence Relief 142
29.1.2.   Partial Residence Relief... 143

29.2.   How Long In A Property Before It Can Be Classed As My PPR? _____ 143

29.3.   More Insight Into What Makes A PPR_____ 144

29.3.1.   Practical Tip... 145

29.4.   Private Residence CGT Exemption - How To Lose It! _____ 145

29.5.   Private Residence Relief – When Relief May Be Restricted _____ 146

29.5.1.   Restriction 1 – Use For Purpose Of A Trade, Business Profession Or Vocation 147
29.5.2.   Restriction 2 – Change Of Use.. 148
29.5.3.   Restriction 3 – Development Gains.. 149

30.   *The 36, 18 And Now 9-Month Rule* 150

30.1.   The Old '36-month Rule' _____ 150

30.2.   The New '18-month Rule' _____ 150

30.3.   The Newer '9-month Rule' _____ 150

31.   *Private Letting Relief* 151

31.1.   The Abolishment Of Private Lettings Relief – April 6th 2020 _____ 152

31.1.1.   Restricted Relief.. 152
31.1.2.   From Bad To Worse… 153

32.   *Increasing Property Value And Avoiding Tax* 155

32.1.   No CGT On The First 12 Months Of Ownership_____ 155

32.2.   Using The Rule To Grow A Portfolio Without Paying CGT _____ 156

33.   *Nominating Residence To Avoid CGT* *157*

   33.1.   **Having More Than One Family Home** _____ 157

   33.2.   **Nominating Your Residence to HMRC** _____ 157

34.   *Other Ways To Reduce Your CGT Bill* *159*

   34.1.   **Using Your Annual CGT Allowance** _____ 159

   34.2.   **Capital Losses** _____ 160

   34.3.   **Buying And Selling Costs** _____ 161

   34.4.   **Selling At The Right Time Can Save You Tax!** _____ 161

35.   *Using Property Partnerships To Cut Your CGT bill* *163*

   35.1.   **Making Use Of Multiple CGT Allowances** _____ 163

   35.2.   **Save Tax By Transferring To Your Husband/Wife Or Civil Partner** _____ 163

      35.2.1.   Transferring To Lower-Rate Taxpayer 163
      35.2.2.   Transferring If Partner Has Registered Losses 164

   35.3.   **Transferring Strategies For Non-spouse And Non-Civil Partnerships** ____ 165

      35.3.1.   Transferring In Stages 165

   35.4.   **Transferring At 'Arm's Length'** _____ 165

   35.5.   **Putting Property Into Joint Names Before Sale** _____ 166

      35.5.1.   No Gain/No Loss Transfers 166
      35.5.2.   Using The Annual Exempt Amount 166
      35.5.3.   Reducing the rate at which tax is paid 167
      35.5.4.   Property Has Been A Main Residence 168
      35.5.5.   Practical Tip 169

36.   *Advanced Strategies For Avoiding CGT* *170*

   36.1.   **How To Claim An Additional Three Years Of PPR** _____ 170

   36.2.   **Claiming PPR When Working Overseas** _____ 171

   36.3.   **Claiming PPR When Re-locating In The UK** _____ 171

   36.4.   **CGT Implications Of Providing Property To Dependent Relatives** _____ 172

37.   *Understanding Inheritance Tax* *173*

   37.1.   **What Is Inheritance Tax?** _____ 173

   37.2.   **One VERY Important Point To Note!** _____ 174

   37.3.   **FOUR Simple Ways To Reduce Inheritance Tax** _____ 174

   37.4.   **Don't Forget Your Capital Gains Liability** _____ 176

   37.5.   **How To Avoid Inheritance Tax On Your Family Home** _____ 176

37.5.1.   Lifetime Planning..177
37.5.2.   "First Death" Planning 178

37.6.   Other IHT Exemptions_____ **179**

37.6.1.   Completely Exempt...179
37.6.2.   Annual Exemptions..179

37.7.   The Residence Nil Rate Band (RNRB) _____ **179**

38.   *How To Better Manage Your Landlord Taxes*.............................*180*

39.   *A Final Reminder - The Golden Tax Rules* *182*
39.1.1.   Education…Education…Education..182
39.1.2.   Prevention Is Better Than Cure..182

1. About The Authors

Some words about the authors of this unique guide, bringing together a property tax specialist and a property investor!

1.1. Arthur Weller - The Property Tax Specialist

Arthur Weller is a tax specialist who advises other accountants. He is one of the most knowledgeable and respected tax specialists in the country.

He is also the lead technical tax specialist and design consultant for www.property-tax-portal.co.uk.

Arthur is based in the northwest and qualified in 1997 as a certified accountant in a small firm of accountants. They specialised to a degree in property, and he worked for some years in their tax department.

He then moved on to a medium-sized firm, where he was the technical manager in the tax department.

In 1998 he passed the exams of the Institute of Taxation, and in June 2000 he left to set up his own tax consultancy.

Arthur works mainly in an advisory capacity for accountants in all areas of taxation. He also runs a telephone help line, giving phone advice on all areas of taxation to accountants around the country.

Much of his work has been focused in the following areas:

- property taxation (Arthur is regarded as a property tax specialist);
- capital gains tax;
- stamp duty;
- income tax;
- company tax;

Arthur has advised over 1,500 landlords, property investors and tax professionals through the Property Tax Portal Consultancy page here:

>> https://www.property-tax-portal.co.uk/consultancy_arthur.shtml

1.2. Amer Siddiq - The Landlord

First and foremost, Amer Siddiq is a UK landlord/property investor. He is passionate about all aspects of property investment and over the last nine years has grown a portfolio in the northwest of England

As well as growing a portfolio and speaking in public at various property investment events, Amer has also brought to market a number of websites to help landlords to better manage and grow their portfolios whilst reducing their taxes.

These include:

landlord vision	**Landlord Vision** Our next generation landlord software solution that runs in the cloud. **Take your FREE Trial today.** Visit: www.landlordvision.co.uk
taxinsider	**Tax Insider** A website providing monthly tax newsletters to help UK tax payers minimise their taxes. Visit: www.taxinsider.co.uk

1.3. Acknowledgements

Lee Sharpe, Chartered Tax Advisor and author of:

- How to Use Companies to Reduce Property Taxes,
- Tax Secrets for Property Developers and Renovators

Both books can be purchased through www.property-tax-portal.co.uk website.

Lee is also a public speaker and provides valuable tax expertise to the www.property-tax-portal.co.uk and www.taxinsider.co.uk websites.

Other acknowledgements include:
- Mark McLaughlin CTA (Fellow) ATT (Fellow) TEP
- Jennifer Adams FCIS TEP ATT (Fellow)- Principal
- Sarah Bradford BA (Hons) ACA CTA (Fellow)
- Alan Pink FCA CTA

2. The Importance Of Tax Planning

We all instinctively do some tax planning in our daily lives, even if it is simply remembering to buy our "duty frees" when we return from our holiday abroad.

If you are going to make the best of your property business, then you need to be alert to the tax implications of your business plans, and to any opportunities to reduce the likely tax bill. Your instinct may be enough for your duty-free goodies, but for tax on your business, you need a more structured approach!

"Tax planning" means arranging your business affairs so that you pay the minimum amount of tax that the law requires. It does not mean trying to conceal things from the Taxman, and it does not mean indulging in highly complex (and expensive!) artificial "tax avoidance" schemes.

"Every man is entitled if he can to order his affairs so that the tax attaching under the appropriate Acts is less than it would otherwise be." That is what the House of Lords said in 1935, when they found for the Duke of Westminster and against the Inland Revenue. This still holds true today, though there is now a mass of "anti-avoidance" legislation to consider when thinking about tax planning – and before you ask, the Duke's tax planning idea was stopped by anti-avoidance legislation!

2.1. Knowing When To Consider Planning

A question you will most certainly ask yourself is 'when should I consider tax planning for my property business?'

The short answer is "all the time", but to be realistic, no-one is likely to do this. The trick is to develop by experience, a sense of when a tax planning opportunity (or a potentially expensive tax pitfall) is likely to present itself.

You should consider tax planning in all of the following situations, for example:

2.1.1. Buying

If you are buying a property, you need to consider:

- Buying the property – It could be you as an individual, you and your spouse, you and a business partner, a Limited Company owned by you, or perhaps a Trust you have set up. Your decision will depend on your future business strategy

- Financing the property – You will need to consider whether you are taking out a mortgage, and if so how will it be secured. It may not always make sense to secure the loan on the property you are buying if you have other assets on which you can secure the loan.

- Plans for the property – It could be that you are you buying the property to sell it again in the short term, or to hold it long term and benefit from the rental income. The tax treatment will be different according to which is the case, and different planning should be done before the property is bought.

2.1.2.   Repairs And Refurbishment

If you spend money on a property, you need to consider:

- Whether you are doing it in order to sell it again in the short term, or whether you will continue letting it.

- If the work being done is classed as a **repair** to the property, or an **improvement.** See icon below for the difference between the two.

The distinction between a repair and an improvement to a property is very important, because although the cost of repairs can be deducted from your rental income for tax purposes, an improvement can only be claimed as a deduction against CGT when you sell the property.

Essentially, a repair is when you replace like with like, whereas an improvement involves adding to the property (say, a conservatory or a loft conversion), or replacing something with something significantly better (say, removing the old storage heaters and installing oil-fired central heating).

HMRC do not always behave logically when it comes to repairs versus improvements.

James Bailey shares the following experience with us:

"A client of mine sold a seaside property, in circumstances where he would have to pay CGT on the sale profit. He had spent a lot of money on this property, which when he bought it had not been touched since the early 1950s.

He had ripped out the old "utility" kitchen, for example, and replaced it with a state-of –the –art designer affair in gleaming slate, chrome, and steel. The old 1950s cooker had had some Bakelite knobs to turn the gas on and off – the new kitchen range had the computer power of the average 1970s space capsule.

Clearly an improvement, and so deductible from his capital gain, but HMRC tried to argue that one kitchen is much like another and he was just replacing like with like – so they said it was a repair, which was no good to him in his case as there was no rental income from which he could deduct the cost of repairs."

2.1.3.   Selling

When you decide to dispose of a property, there are other tax issues to consider:

- Who is the property going to? – If it is to someone "connected" with you, such as a close relative or a business partner, and if you do not charge them the full market value, HMRC can step in and tax you as if you had sold it for full value.

- Will you be paying CGT or income tax on the profit you make? – The planning opportunities are very different, depending on which tax is involved.

- What are the terms of the sale? Is it just a cash sale, or is the buyer a developer who is offering you a "slice of the action" in the form of a share of the profits from the development? There is important anti-avoidance legislation to consider if this is the case.

2.1.4. Life Changes

Whenever your life undergoes some significant changes, you should consider tax planning.

Here are some examples when tax planning should be considered:

- Getting married – a married couple (and a civil partnership) have a number of tax planning opportunities denied to single people, but there are also one or two pitfalls to watch out for.

- Moving house – it is usually not a good idea to sell the old house immediately, as there are often tax advantages to keeping it and letting it out.

- Changing your job. You may become a higher or lower rate tax payer, and this may mean you should change your tax strategy.

  If you are moving house, and you sell the old residence, you will have the cash left after you have paid off the mortgage and the various removal costs to spend on your new home. If you need a mortgage to buy the new home, the interest on that mortgage is not allowed as a deduction for tax purposes.

  If, instead, you remortgage the old house and let it out, ALL the mortgage interest you pay can be deducted against the rent you receive (subject to the new rules for interest paid by residential landlords) whatever you do with the cash you have released – and you may well be able to sell the house after nine months of letting (or sometimes a longer period), and pay no CGT on the increased value since you stopped living there.

- Death – IHT is charged at 40% on the value of your estate when you die, to the extent that the value is greater than (for 2020/21) £325,000. By planning early enough it is possible to reduce the IHT burden considerably.

2.1.5. Politics

There are two occasions each year when you need to be particularly alert – the Budget Report in the Autumn, and The Spring Statement in March.

On both these occasions the Chancellor of the Exchequer announces tax rates, and new tax legislation, which might well affect you and your property business. In some cases, however, new tax legislation is announced at other times – it pays to keep a weather eye on the financial pages of the newspaper, or to subscribe to a magazine or journal that will alert you to important tax changes that may affect your business.

2.1.6. End And Start Of The Tax Year

The tax year ends on the 5th April each year and it is a good idea to review your tax situation before this date to make sure you are not missing any planning opportunities.

2.2. The Real Benefits Of Tax Planning

Robert Kiyosaki, author of the number one bestselling book 'Rich Dad Poor Dad', says *'Every time people try to punish the rich, the rich don't simply comply, they react. They have the money, power and intent to change things. They do not sit there and voluntarily pay more taxes. They search for ways to minimize their tax burden'*

The whole purpose of tax planning is to save you tax and to put more profits in your pocket. That is why the rich are always looking at ways of beating the taxman, because they benefit from tax planning.

2.2.1. Paying Less Tax

When I (co-author Amer) started investing in property the challenge to me was not to just grow a property portfolio but to grow it in the most tax efficient way possible.

It soon dawned on me that implementing just the simplest of tax saving strategies was going to help me to make considerably more profits.

Don't fall into the trap where you only think about tax when you are considering selling or even worse after you have sold the property.

By taking tax advice at the right times and on a regular basis you will legitimately avoid or reduce taxes both in the short and the long term.

This means that you will have greater profits to spend as you wish.

2.2.2. Clear 'Entrance' And 'Exit' Strategies

When you sit down and analyse properties that you are considering for investment, you will no doubt look at how much rental income the property will generate and what you expect to achieve in capital appreciation.

Knowing the estimated tax liabilities right from the outset will save you from any nasty surprises in the future.

> Your personal circumstances can change at a whim. The last thing that you want to do is fall into a situation where you are forced to sell a property but are unable to pay the taxman because you never considered your tax situation.

2.2.3. Staying Focused

When you are deciding on the property investment strategies that you are going to adopt it is a good idea to talk them through with a tax adviser.

If your investment strategy changes then it is likely to have an impact on your tax strategy, so it should be reviewed with your tax adviser.

Your tax strategy will go hand in hand with your investment strategy and will help you to keep focused on your property investment and financial goals.

2.2.4.   Improving Cash Flow

One of the challenges that you will face as a property investor is cash flow. In other words, you need to make sure that you have enough money coming in from your property business to pay for all property related bills, maintenance and repairs, and of course tax on the rental profits.

> Remember, timing of expenditures can be the difference between a 'high' and a 'nil' tax bill. Therefore, keeping in regular contact with your tax adviser, especially when coming towards the end of the tax year can have a significant impact on your property cash flow.

2.2.5.   Avoiding Common Tax Traps

There are many tax traps that you can fall into if you have not taken any tax advice at all, not to mention the numerous great tax planning opportunities you will miss out on too. It is not uncommon to hear stories about investors who have made a £100,000 profit on a single property and then sold it without taking any tax advice whatsoever. If you fall into this situation, then you could be hit with a hefty tax bill.

It will hurt you even more if after selling you realise that you could have easily turned the tax liability to zero had you taken some simple tax advice.

Good tax advisers will know of the most common traps that you are likely to fall into, so a few minutes spent wisely could save you thousands in taxes.

2.3.   Asking HMRC For Tax Advice

From time to time people tell the TaxInsider.co.uk office that all the effort that goes into offering them tax advice is a waste of time, and tax consultants are also unnecessary, because you can simply telephone HM Revenue & Customs (HMRC) and get free advice. However, free advice is not always the best advice.

2.3.1.   Making Use Of HMRC Services

Getting advice from HMRC in some circumstances is always a good idea – for example, they operate a number of "clearance" services whereby you can set out the details of a proposed transaction for them, and they will tell you the tax consequences they believe will flow from it.

Some of these clearances are enshrined in statute – there are some quite draconian examples of anti-avoidance legislation which can also catch quite innocent commercial transactions, and there is a statutory process for obtaining HMRC's agreement in advance that they will not wheel out their sledgehammers to crack your innocent commercial nut.

There are also other informal HMRC clearance procedures which can be useful when you are considering a transaction where the tax treatment may turn on a matter of opinion, and it is useful to know HMRC's opinion in advance.

It is also possible to agree valuations of assets for capital gains tax purposes where these are needed to complete a tax return – much better to have the discussion before you put the return in than to hope for the best and submit it, only to have the same discussion as part of an HMRC "Aspect Enquiry" where the possibility of penalties looms if they consider your valuation was a little sloppy!

Tax specialists use such services frequently on behalf of clients, and they are a great help in providing a better service for them.

2.3.2.   The Drawback

However, the "help" that the people who contact Tax Insider are referring to is the "help" you can get by ringing HMRC up while filling in your tax return, or when confronted by a tax situation that you do not understand. In some cases, no harm will result, and you may even get the right answer, but on the whole professional advisors am very nervous about this "Do it yourself" approach to tax.

HMRC's own policy on giving advice is contained in their "Code of Practice 10", and the following sentence from that document illustrates a major gap in their service:

"However, we will not help with tax planning, or advise on transactions designed to avoid or reduce the tax charge which might otherwise be expected to arise".

2.3.3.   Practical Tip

There is a serious point here – HMRC do their best to promote the view that there is a "correct" amount of tax that is due as a result of any particular transaction, whereas in all but the simplest of cases, there are grey areas and the way a transaction is structured can make a big difference to the resulting tax bill.

As Lord Tomlin said in the House of Lords during the case of The Duke of Westminster v The Commissioners of Inland Revenue in 1936 *"Every man is entitled if he can to order his affairs so that the tax attaching under the appropriate Acts is less than it would otherwise be"*.

That remains good law and seems to me a sensible way to deal with the State's demands for ever higher taxes, but don't expect HMRC to help you!

3. Making Tax Digital For Landlords

On 18 March 2015 under the heading of 'Making Tax Easier', the then Chancellor, George Osborne, announced that the chore of submitting annual self-assessment tax returns by 31 January was to be abolished. There were loud cheers from back benchers but it is only now that the full impact of the changes is being understood. The initiative has been given the title 'Making Tax Digital' (MTD) and is one of the biggest changes made to the UK tax system for generations. It will affect all taxpayers, including landlords.

3.1.   What Is Making Tax Digital?

'Making Tax Digital' (MTD) has been described as one of the biggest changes made to the UK tax system for generations. It will eventually affect all taxpayers, including landlords.

The two key requirements for MTD are to:

- keep transaction records via a 'digital link' and
- use compatible software to submit returns to HMRC

HMRC are looking for 'transparency' between the underlying accounting records of the business and tax returns; this, HMRC believes, will reduce the risk of tax error, making compliance and enforcement more efficient.

Under the MTD system, taxpayers will no longer submit returns by totalling figures manually, completing the return by hand and sending to HMRC by post or by loading directly onto the taxpayers' own Government Gateway account and submitting. Instead transactions will be required to be recorded digitally and the detail submitted using MTD compatible software. The software will electronically link bookkeeping records into HMRC's MTD computers. HMRC will not be providing software to enable submissions and as such landlords will be compelled to use commercially produced software to submit.

The use of spreadsheets will still be permitted and for a spreadsheet to be MTD compliant the initial input of data will need to be keyed in manually and then any further transfer, recapture or modification of that same data will be completed using digital links (termed 'bridging' software).

NOTE: Landlord Vision is now recognised by HMRC as an MTD ready software and is currently in the alpha testing phase.

3.2.   What Has Changed?

No changes are being made to:

- the underlying tax rules;
- the level of detail of information required to be submitted which will remain the same as the current self assessment tax return, or
- the current payment deadlines for income tax.

However, there will be changes to the number of returns (termed 'updates') submitted and submission dates.

3.3.   Submission Dates

The annual tax return submitted every year by 31 January is to be abolished, instead taxpayers will be required to submit 'updates' on a quarterly basis (or more frequently if the taxpayer so wishes). There will also be a final submission termed an 'end of year activity' report applying 9 months after the fourth quarter. This last submission will confirm the previous submissions and include claims such as the restriction of mortgage interest, (if such information has not already been included in the 'updates') and so, in effect, there will be five submissions per tax year in total. The 'time window' for submission will be from 10 days before the quarter end to one month after.

3.3.1.   Real Time Basis

In the consultation document that HMRC issued on the intended workings of MTD, it was stated that: *'Updating HMRC quarterly and more frequently if the business desires will ensure the tax system operates on a 'near real time' basis'.*

When an 'update' is submitted, HMRC's computer will calculate the taxpayer's potential tax bill in as close to 'real time' as possible and at the same time remind (termed 'prompt') the taxpayer of the dates of payment; the idea being that this will aid taxpayers to pay the correct amount of tax, putting a stop to underpayments or overpayments.

This system will enable taxpayers to view and manage their tax information in one place via an online digital account similar to the way that accounts can be viewed on a bank screen online. The intention is for each taxpayer to be able to view their current ('real time') tax liabilities whichever type of tax is paid in one place via the Government Gateway and even have the ability to enable offset of overpayments in one tax against underpayments in others.

3.4.   When Is MTD Starting?

3.4.1.   Stage 1

MTD is being introduced in stages. The first set of taxpayers to submit under the new system were those businesses that were compulsorily registered for VAT (including those furnished holiday let businesses so registered) and whose VAT quarter ended on 30 June 2019. These businesses therefore submitted their first MTD 'update' on 7 August 2019.

The remaining VAT registered businesses joined when their respective return was subsequently due. HMRC offered a 'soft landing period' to enable businesses to make the transfer from manual to digital without penalty. This 'period' was set to end on either 1 April 2020 or 1 October 2020 depending on when the business first registered for MTD for VAT.

However, in light of the Covid-19 pandemic, HMRC has extended this 'period' such that all businesses now have until their first VAT return period starting on or after 1 April 2021 to put digital links in place.

The impact of additional submissions will not be as hard felt for these VAT registered businesses as for other taxpayers because these businesses are already used to submitting more than one return a year. However, for other taxpayers the additional submission requirements may prove to be an increased chore.

3.4.2.   Stages 2 And 3

The second 'roll out' stage will be MTD for income tax for the self-employed and landlords. The third and final stage will be MTD for corporation tax when all non VAT registered companies will be expected to comply.

The timetable for MTD for income tax has been amended several times. The governments' announcement of the extension of full digitalisation for compulsorily VAT registered businesses will almost certainly mean that stages two and three will also be delayed. The most recent announcement with reference to the introduction of MTD for income tax was made in March 2019 wherein it was announced that the system would not be introduced until *'at least 2021'*.

In March 2020 HMRC issued a document titled *"Making Tax Digital: An evaluation of the VAT service and update on the Income Tax Service"*. In that document HMRC evaluated the effectiveness and progress of the MTD for VAT programme and confirmed that they remained intent on implementing MTD for income tax. In the document HMRC confirmed that they would be building on the experiences and lessons learned with the implementation of MTD for VAT.

As such it will, of course, be prudent for landlords to be aware of the changes that are taking place, in preparation for mandatory MTD for income tax.

3.5.   Which Landlords Will Be Affected?

When MTD for income tax is implemented landlords with less than £10,000 annual income will be exempt - everyone else will have no choice but to comply. The £10,000 income figure is the income from all of the properties and not the profit figure. For landlords who are both self employed and receive rental income, it is likely that income from all sources will be taken into account when ascertaining whether the £10,000 de minimus limit has been reached but this has not been confirmed by HMRC. If the landlord is employed as well as having rental income then the employment income will not be counted towards the £10,000.

Certain exemptions may be made for the small minority of taxpayers who are unable to use digital tools due to their religion, age or disability. There is also likely to be an exemption for those who are affected by low internet speeds (Under 2 mb/s).

3.6.   MTD Compliance

3.6.1.   All Landlords

Although there will be no requirement to submit actual invoices or receipts, this information must still be kept. HMRC would like taxpayers to use software sophisticated enough to scan receipts such that the details are automatically loaded into the chosen software. They believe that this method of 'capture' will reduce the need for manual loading (and as such 'mistakes') and the time incurred in creating quarterly submissions. However, such sophisticated software costs and HMRC have backed away from insisting that this type of software is used.

Submissions will be of total figures only and HMRC's intention is to use the same standard expense headings as are already used on the Property pages of the current tax return.

3.6.2.   Multiple Properties

Where multiple properties are held within a property business, rental income and expenditure will have to be recorded for the business as a whole rather than be shown per individual property. There will, however, be a requirement to maintain details of each property's address in the digital records. If supplies/information is received from third parties (e.g. letting agents) as a summary then those summary figures can be entered into the software as though it were a single invoice.

3.6.3.   Jointly Owned Properties

Currently, each individual provides information on their own tax return detailing their share of the rental income and allowable expenses. This procedure will remain where a property is jointly owned, each individual being required to keep digital records for their share of income and expenditure.

3.6.4.   How And When Will Tax Payments Be Made?

HMRC do not currently plan to change the dates by which payments are made under MTD, remaining at 31 January and 31 July as required although a business will be permitted to make voluntary payments towards their tax liabilities. Such voluntary payments may be made at the discretion of the business and at intervals of their choosing.

3.7.   The New System Of Penalties

Alongside the introduction of MTD, HMRC has said that it will introduce a new penalty regime where businesses fail to comply with filing obligations.

The proposals are for:

- Late filing: a points-based system similar to the current regime for driving offences. Once a certain number of points have been accumulated, a financial penalty will be imposed.
- Late payment: no penalties if tax is paid within 15 days, increased penalties as further time elapses.
- Filing a VAT return other than electronically without the prior agreement of HMRC could produce a penalty, the maximum fine being £400.

NOTE: these proposals have now been postponed. They were omitted from the Finance Act 2019 and it is now anticipated that the new system will be postponed until after April 2021. As such, the current regime remains.

3.8.   Current Penalty System

3.8.1.   VAT Registered Furnished Holiday Lets

In practice, HMRC has not been treating failure to file digitally as being a default which would normally initiate a surcharge period. It is only non or late filings that are covered by the 'soft landing' period, late payments are not covered and as such default surcharge penalties could be levied.

3.8.2.   Other Landlords

Should the self assessment tax return be submitted up to three months after the deadline date of 31 Jan following the tax year, a fixed penalty of £100 is levied. Further fixed and tax geared penalties are charged if the return remains unsubmitted.

Tax geared penalties are levied on payments made 30 days late. Interest is charged on late payments.

3.9.   Simplified 'Cash Basis' For Unincorporated Property Businesses

As part of the changes being brought in by MTD, the way that unincorporated property businesses account for their property income has changed. These changes make the 'cash basis' of accounting the default option where the receipts of that business are less than £150,000 (unless the business elects to use the 'accruals basis').

The 'cash basis' is used to account for income and expenses when the income is received and expenses are paid. The current general disallowance of capital expenditure under the 'cash basis' is replaced by a more specific disallowance for certain assets. The 'accruals basis' accounts for income over the period to which it relates and for expenses in the period in which the liability is incurred.

3.10.   Current Situation

The primary legislation for MTD was contained in the Finance (No.2) Act 2017, with secondary legislation for VAT laid in February 2018. No further legislation has been introduced due to Brexit and the Corona Virus taking precedence.

3.11.   Possible Timetable For 2021/22

No confirmation as to the commencement date for MTD for income tax has been announced and as previously stated what dates have been given have been deferred. However, should the first year for landlords be 2021/22; the potential deadlines would be as follows:

- 1st 'update' 2021/22 - submit June/July 2021.
- 2nd 'update' 2021/22 - submit Sept/Oct 2021
- 3rd 'update' 2021/22 - submit Dec 2021/Jan 2022
- 2020/21 Self Assessment tax return - submit by 31 January 2022

- 4th 'update' 2021/22- submit March/April 2022
- 1st 'update' 2022/23 - submit June/July 2022
- 2nd 'update' 2022/23 - submit Sept/Oct 2022
- 3rd 'update' 2022/23 - submit Dec 2022/Jan 2023
- 5th and final 'end of year activity' 2021/22 - submit January 2023

3.12.   Final Points

HMRC believes that MTD will 'help to reduce arithmetical errors, for example when data is taken out of one system and entered into another. MTD will make it easier for businesses to manage their tax and will save time which can instead be devoted to maximising business opportunities, encouraging growth and fostering good financial planning.' HMRC is of the view that such 'mathematical errors' are errors in the taxpayers" favour and by not making such errors this will mean an increase in the amount of tax HMRC collects.

In addition, over time, the information submitted will create a picture of a taxpayer's business, which will enable HMRC to make more accurate comparisons with other similar businesses than are currently available, which will mean more targeted enquiries.

Critics of the new initiative are not as confident that tax receipts will increase but what is certain is that MTD for landlords will be implemented at some date in the near future.

3.13.   Invest   In   Landlord Software

Landlord vision is a cloud-based property management software intended for busy landlords who need to be able to manage their properties on the go and do the essential administration and finances quickly and efficiently.

Visit: www.landlordvision.co.uk

Knowing Your Property Tax Strategy

4. Understanding Your Tax Liabilities

Over the past few years property investment has become a very profitable way to make money.

Unfortunately, there are very few people who consider the tax implications of their investment strategy before they decide to invest. Instead they take a view that they will address the tax issues when they decide to dispose of the property. This can be a very costly mistake as some simple planning can help to avoid large tax bills in the future.

The table below gives an indication of the tax that may be due if you follow any of the popular strategies outlined below.

Strategy	Description	Income Tax	Capital Gains Tax
Buy-to-let	Probably the most popular investment method and a strategy for long-term investment. Income tax will be due on the annual rental profits and CGT due when the property is disposed of.	Yes	Yes
Develop & Sell	This is typically classed as a short-term (i.e. 3-6 months) investment and only Income Tax is due if you are trading in properties in this way. All property development related expenditures can be offset against the final selling price.	Yes	No
Develop & Rent	Another typical long-term investment, where the property is developed and then rented out. All capital expenditure incurred developing the property can be offset when the property is disposed.	Yes	Yes

	However rental profit will be subject to annual income tax.		
Buy & Sell	If you are a master or want to become a master of buying undervalued property and then re-selling at a higher price, then you will be classed as a property trader and will typically be subject to Income Tax only.	Yes	No
Buy-let-live	A good investment strategy to make use of some very significant tax breaks if you are sitting on large capital gains. This strategy only really applies to investors who intent to hold only a small number of properties during their life-time i.e. (3-6 properties). Again, income tax will be due on rental profits and CGT when the property is disposed of.	Yes	Yes (but is dramatically reduced)
Buy-live-let	Probably the most tax efficient way to avoid capital gains tax for the small investor. This increasingly popular strategy involves letting your previous main residence when buying a new home or moving abroad. Again, income tax will be due on rental profits and CGT when the property is disposed of.	Yes	Yes (but is dramatically reduced)
Rent-a-Room	If you decide to rent-a-room that is part of your main residence then you can receive an annual rental income, to the value of £7,500 and not have any income tax liability. Ay income above this amount will be subject to income tax. CGT is not due if you sell your main residence which has been	Yes (if claiming rent-a-room relief and income is greater than £7,500)	No (if tenants live with the family owning the property)

	classed as your only home during the whole period of ownership. Please Note: if the tenants renting do not live together with the family, then there can be CGT on that part of the house rented out. See section 23 for more details		
Furnished Holiday Lets	If you let a furnished property as a holiday let, then you will be subject to income tax on any rental profits. There are number of very generous tax breaks available for those investing in Furnished Holiday Lets. See section 24 for more details	Yes	Yes

How To Slash Your Property Income Tax

Before we look at the different income tax saving strategies, it is important to understand what is meant by the term **income tax** and when property investors and landlords are liable to pay it.

5. Income Tax Liabilities For Investors/Traders

Anybody investing in property is liable to pay income tax on any profitable income that is generated from their properties.

There are two main categories of people who invest in property, and both are liable to pay income tax. The characteristics of each are detailed in the following sections.

5.1. Property Investor

If you invest in property for the long term, i.e., you have buy-to-let properties, then you will be referred to as a **property investor** (more commonly known as a landlord). This is because you are holding on to a property for the long term.

If you are letting your investment properties, then you will be liable to pay income tax annually on the rental profits.

It is also likely that you will have another source of income, unless you have a large portfolio of properties where the rental income funds your lifestyle.

5.2. Property Traders/Dealers

If you are investing in property for the short term, i.e., 6–12 months, and intend to sell with the aim of generating a dealing profit, then you will be referred to as **property dealer** or **property trader**.

Property dealers and traders are liable to pay income tax when they sell the property.

You will find that most full-time property developers or renovators are classed as property dealers/traders.

5.3. Income Tax Rates

You can use the following link to view the income tax rates for previous years:

http://www.hmrc.gov.uk/rates/it.htm

The current rates of income tax for the 2020–2021 tax year are detailed in the table below:

INCOME TAX 2020–2021

Rate	Band	Description
Nil	£0 to £12,500	The first £12,500 of each individual's income is Tax Free.
20%	£12,501 to £50,000	The next £37,500 is taxed at 20%.
40%	£50,001 to £100,000	The next £50,000 is taxed at 40%.
60%	£100,001 to £125,000	The next £25,000 is taxed at 60%. This is because of the withdrawal of the Personal Allowance.
40%	£ 125,001 to 150,000	The next £25,000 is taxed at 40%.
45%	> £150,000	Anything above £150,000 is taxed at 45%

The above table assumes that the personal allowance is £12,500. It also disregards the 0% tax rate on savings income for the first £5,000.

5.4.   Income Tax Calculation Case Studies

Here are some case studies to illustrate how the tax liability is calculated for property investors and property dealers/traders.

5.4.1.   Income Tax Calculation For Property Investors

The case study below illustrates the income tax liability for a basic-rate taxpayer.

Income Tax Calculation for Property Investor (1)

John works as a local government officer and receives an annual salary of £20,000. He buys a property close to his local hospital for £95,000. He receives a monthly rental income of £600.

The property is let for the whole 2020–2021 tax year, which means that he has received an annual rental income of £7,200.

In the tax year he has also incurred property-related expenses of £1,400.

These expenditures are made up as follows:

Expense	Amount
Insurance £600	
Plumbing (to fix water leak)	£150
Annual gas safety inspection	£100
Central heating maintenance contract	£300
Replacement door fitted	£250
Total Expenditure	£1,400

This means that John's taxable rental profit is £5,800 (i.e., £7,200 – £1,400).

On this amount he is liable to pay tax at 20%. This is because his £5,800 rental profit falls into the basic rate band.

Therefore, his tax liability is **£1,160** on the £5,800 profit.

The following case study illustrates how the rental income from the property pushes John into the higher-rate tax band.

Income Tax Calculation for Property Investor (2)

This is the same scenario as in the previous case study. The only difference is that John has an annual salary of £48,150.

John's tax liability on the £5,800 profit is now calculated as follows.

The first £1,850 is taxed at the basic rate of 20%.

The remaining £3,950 is taxed at the higher rate of 40%. This is because the rental profit has taken his total income into the higher-rate tax band.

Therefore, his tax liability is as follows:

$$(£1,850 \times 0.2) + \quad (£3,950 \times 0.4)$$
$$£370 \quad + \quad £1,580$$

$$= \quad £1.950$$

John's tax liability is **£1,950** on the £5,200 profit.

5.4.2. Income Tax Calculation For Property Developers

It is important to remember that if you become a property dealer, then this is a new self-employed trade and you are liable for Class 4 National Insurance (NI) on the profits as well as for Class 2 NI. See HMRC leaflet SE1 Thinking of working for yourself:
www.gov.uk/government/uploads/system/uploads/attachment_data/file/366588/se1.pdf.

In order to make the case studies in this section easier to understand the NI contributions have not been calculated.

The following case study illustrates how the income tax liability is calculated for a part-time property dealer.

Income Tax Calculation for Property Dealer (1)

Bill works as a local government officer and earns a salary of £31,000. Bill wants to become a property developer, so he buys a run-down property for £50,000 in December 2018.

He spends £20,000 renovating and re-decorating the property before selling it six months later for £95,000.

This gives him a taxable profit of £25,000 (i.e. selling price – (purchase price + costs incurred on the property)).

Bill's tax liability on the £25,000 profit is made in the 2019–2020 tax year, so his tax liability is calculated as follows.

The first £19,000 is taxed at the basic rate of 20%.

The remaining £6,000 is taxed at the higher rate of 40%. This is because the property development profit has taken his total income into the higher-rate tax band.

Therefore, his tax liability is as follows:

$$(£19,000 \times 0.2) \quad + \quad (£6,000 \times 0.4)$$
$$£3,800 \quad\quad\quad + \quad\quad £2,400$$
$$= \quad £6,200$$

Bill's tax liability is **£6,200** on the £25,000 profit.

The following case study illustrates how the income tax liability is calculated for a full-time property dealer.

Income Tax Calculation for Property Dealer (2)

Robert, a colleague of Bill and John, resigns from his job in the local government and decides to become a full-time property dealer.

In his first year of dealing he buys two properties, renovates them, and sells them for a profit of £55,000 each. This means that he has a taxable income of £110,000. The profit is made in the 2019–2020 tax year, so his tax liability is calculated as follows.

- The first £12,500 is tax-free due to the personal allowance.
- The next £37,500 is taxed at the basic rate of 20%.
- The next £50,000 is taxed at the rate of 40%.
- The remaining £10,000 is taxed at the even higher rate of 60%.

Here is the tax calculation:

Tax Rate	Amount	Tax Liability
Nil	£12,500	£0
20%	£37,500	£7,500
40%	£50,000	£20,000
60%	£10,000	£6,000
Total Tax Liability		**£33,500**

Therefore, Robert has a tax liability of **£33,500** on the £110,000 profit.

6.   Owning Properties As A Sole Trader

Holding a property in a sole name can be tax beneficial under certain circumstances.

In this section we will get to grips with why people hold properties as a sole trader and will learn about some of the tax benefits and drawbacks of owning properties in this way.

6.1.   Buying Properties As A Sole Trader

A **sole trader** is an individual who buys properties in his or her sole name.

Although it is still a very common way to purchase properties, it is not necessarily the most tax efficient.

In most cases, properties are usually purchased as a sole trader for non-tax-related reasons.

Here are the two most common non-tax-related reasons why you might decide to buy property as a sole trader.

a)   You don't have a partner who you can invest with.

b)   You don't want to invest with anybody else; that is, you can't trust anybody, or you want total control over your investment.

If you have invested for either of these reasons, then you can still make tax savings.

6.2.   When Is It Tax Efficient To Buy Property As A Sole Trader?

The ideal scenario for buying a property as a sole trader is if you have no other income.

The reason for this is because you can utilise your annual, tax-free personal allowance.

In simple terms, the further your income is from the higher-rate tax bands, the more you will save in income tax by having the property in your sole name. This is especially true if your partner is a higher-rate taxpayer.

The following two case studies illustrate these points.

Sole Trader With No Income

Joanne is a married woman but does not work. Her husband is a high-flying executive who earns £70,000 per annum.

Upon the death of a relative, Joanne is left £100,000. She uses the entirety of this inheritance to purchase an investment property.

She makes £600 rental profit per month. (She bought the property with cash, so therefore she has no outstanding mortgage or other costs in the 2019-20 tax year).

This means that she makes an annual rental profit of £7,200.

She is not liable to pay any tax on this amount as it is within the annual personal income tax allowance of £12,500.

Had Joanne bought the property in joint ownership with her husband, then he would have been liable to pay tax at 40% on his share of the investment. If his share of the property was 50%, then he would have an annual tax liability of £1,440.

This means that over a 10-year period, Joanne will see a minimum tax saving of £14,400 by owning the property in her sole name.

Property Investor With No Income, but Partner Works

Chris is married and earns £15,000 per annum as a store sales assistant. His wife runs a pharmacy and earns £45,000 per annum.

They decide that they want to start investing in property and purchase a property for £45,000.

They take tax advice before investing and are told that they will pay less annual income tax if the property is purchased in Chris's sole name.

This is because he is not a higher-rate taxpayer.

6.3.   When Is It NOT Tax Efficient To Buy Property As A Sole Trader?

Try not to buy property as a sole trader if you are a higher-rate taxpayer i.e. paying tax at 40%, 45% or even 60%, especially if you can invest with a partner who is a lower-rate taxpayer.

If you are a higher-rate taxpayer, then you will have to pay income tax on any rental income at the higher rate as well.

It would be very poor tax planning on your end if you ended up paying 40%, 45% or 60% tax on all rental income, especially if you had a partner who could make use of the nil rate band or the 20% tax band.

6.4. A Note About Selling Properties When Operating As A Sole Trader

You now know when it is beneficial to buy properties as a sole trader.

However, it is generally better to have a property in a joint name when you come to sell the property. The main exception to this rule is if the property has been your PPR; see section 27 for further details.

7. Income Tax & Property Partnerships

There is no doubt that owning properties in a partnership can be an excellent income tax–saving strategy.

In this section you will learn how owning properties in partnerships can significantly reduce your income tax bill.

7.1. What Is A Property Partnership?

To put it simply, a property partnership exists when two or more people own a property in joint names.

When a property is held as a partnership, it is usually held in either of the following two ways.

7.1.1. Joint Tenants

This method is most commonly used when a husband and wife purchase a property together.

The most important point about this method of ownership is that when one of the joint tenants dies, the surviving tenant becomes the sole owner.

Owning Properties as Joint Tenants

Lisa and Alex are husband and wife and own a property as joint tenants. Unfortunately, Lisa passes away due to ill health.

The property now automatically becomes the sole ownership of Alex, without the need to wait for grant of probate or administration.

7.1.2. Tenants In Common

This method is used when the owners of the property want to register the fact that they have separate ownership. This method is most commonly used when two or more unconnected people purchase a property together.

The most important point to note about this method is that when one of the 'tenants in common' dies, the property does not necessarily become the ownership of the surviving tenants.

Owning Properties as 'Tenants in Common'

Jack and Bill are two long-term friends who decide to start investing in properties together.

They are also both married.

Jack is the wealthier of the two, so when they decide to purchase a property, he funds 60% of the deposit. Therefore, it is agreed that the property will be a 60:40 split in Jack's favour.

They purchase the property as 'tenants in common,' where they specify that the property will be passed to their estate should either party die.

Jack is the first to pass away. Upon his death, his 60% ownership in the property is passed to his wife.

7.2.   When To Consider Buying In A Partnership

As we saw in section 6, you should generally try to avoid owning a property as a sole trader if you are a higher-rate taxpayer. This is purely because you will be liable to pay tax at the higher rate on any profitable rental income.

The two most important conditions that must be satisfied before investing with a partner are that:

a) your partner must be a lower rate taxpayer than yourself; that is, if you pay tax at 40%. 45% or 60%, then your partner should pay tax at 20% or less;

b) you MUST be able to trust your partner(s).

> If you are already a nil-rate taxpayer, then don't go looking for a partner who is a higher-rate taxpayer.

This is because you will be unnecessarily passing on an income tax liability to your partner.

Instead, consider keeping the property in your sole name until your rental profits lead you to incur a tax liability at a rate that is equal to or greater than that of your partner.

7.3.   Partners Must Be TRUSTWORTHY

If you buy property in a partnership, then you MUST make sure that the partners with whom you are purchasing are people who you **implicitly** trust, e.g., a spouse, your mother, your father, etc.

This is not just for tax reasons; it is simply good **BUSINESS PRACTICE**.

7.4.   Partnerships Between Husband And Wife

> HMRC will treat all properties purchased between husband and wife (other than shares in a close company) as a 50:50 split, unless otherwise stated.

In fact, HMRC treat all jointly owned property between husband and wife as an equal 50:50 split, unless otherwise stated.

This means that unless you tell HMRC otherwise, you will both be taxed 50:50 on any property rental profits.

A considerable amount of tax can be saved by having a property jointly owned by husband and wife, especially if one or the other is a nil- or a lower-rate taxpayer. It is important to note that if you intend to have a property between husband and wife as a non-50:50 split, then you must have an agreement between the two of you to say that this is the case.

It is not enough to just make a declaration to HMRC stating that a property is owned in unequal shares. It must actually be owned in this manner, and documentary evidence must be made available if requested by HMRC.

The following case study illustrates this scenario along with considerable tax savings.

Potential Tax Savings Between Husband and Wife

After five years of marital bliss, John and Lisa decide to buy an investment property.

John is a 40% tax payer, whereas Lisa is a homemaker and therefore has no income.

They buy a two-bedroom terraced house for £80,000. They decide to have the property as a 90:10 split between the two of them in favour of Lisa and produce documentary evidence to support this. They also inform HMRC of this split.

(The property is split in this manner to take advantage of Lisa's personal income tax allowance—in other words, they want to reduce their tax bill!)

They make £6,000 rental profit on the property on an annual basis. This means that the profit is split as follows:

- Lisa's share of the profit is £5,400;
- John's share of the profit is £600.

Lisa has no tax liability as her profit is within her tax allowance, and John pays £240 tax on his £600 profit.

If the property had remained as a 50:50 split, then the total joint tax liability would have been £1,200 (i.e. 40% of John's £3,000 share).

Therefore, they have an annual savings of £960! Over 10 years, this gives tax savings of at least £9,600.

7.5. Partnerships Between Those Other Than A Husband And Wife

If a property is purchased as a partnership between those other than a husband and wife, you **MUST** inform HMRC of the split.

In this type of partnership HMRC do not make any assumptions as to how the property is split. It is the taxpayer's duty to tell HMRC how the property has been split, and it must be based on fact.

For example, if you buy a property in a partnership with a friend, in which he or she provides 70% of the deposit and you provide 30% of the deposit, then you must also inform HMRC of the 70:30 split.

7.6. How To Declare A Partnership Split to HMRC

If you are a husband and wife wanting an unequal split, then you must make a declaration to HMRC about the ownership split.

Such a declaration takes effect from the date it is made, providing notice of the declaration is given to HMRC via Form 17 within 60 days.

If you would like to download a copy of Form 17, please visit the following link:

>> http://www.hmrc.gov.uk/forms/form17.pdf

It is important to note that the form only covers the assets listed on it. This means that if you have other properties that you want to be covered by the Form 17, they must also be listed to make HMRC aware of split.

Evidence of the ownership of the asset should also be provided to HMRC together with Form 17.

Please note that different HMRC offices differ with regards to what evidence is required to prove the ownership split for a property.

There are two common ways to prove the split.

   a) Provide a signed declaration by the two parties concerned detailing that ownership of the joint property is split in a specific way.

This is acceptable to some HMRC officers.

However, other officers will want more formal proof.

b) Provide more formal property documents that include the following:
   i.   the deeds of conveyance;
   ii. bank accounts (to see letters to and from the bank confirming the change).

The best thing is just to send in (a), but be prepared to send in (b) if HMRC requires it or asks any further questions.

7.7.   Moving Properties Into Joint Ownership To Avoid Income Tax

If you have realised from this strategy that you can save tax by holding your property in a partnership, then you may well be thinking about how to transfer to joint ownership.

Well, it is actually very easy to do, and you will incur *no* capital gains tax liability if you are transferring part ownership to your spouse, i.e., your husband or wife.

PLEASE NOTE: If part ownership of the property is to be transferred to anybody other than your spouse, then there may be a capital gains tax liability triggered.

7.7.1.   Three Simple Steps To Follow

The following three steps will show you how you can transfer the property into joint ownership.

STEP 1. Contact your mortgage lender.

Tell your mortgage lender that you want to transfer the property into joint ownership, and explain why you want to do this.

Your mortgage lender will then send you a new mortgage application form for you to complete in order to move the property into joint ownership.

Unfortunately, lenders will treat transferring an existing property into joint ownership as though you are applying for a new mortgage. Therefore, it is very likely that you will have to submit the same paperwork again and effectively apply for a new mortgage.

It is likely that the property will be put into joint names on the same terms as the original contract; that is, if the original mortgage was fixed at 4.99% and had four years left to run on the fixed period, then the new mortgage will also be the same.

However, if mortgage rates have reduced, then be cheeky and ask if you can also have it at the new reduced interest rate!

STEP 2. Contact a solicitor.

Once your mortgage application has been approved, your solicitor can have all relevant documents changed into joint names pretty quickly. It usually takes about four weeks to complete all the legal paperwork.

Also, tell your solicitor whether you want the property to be owned as 'Joint Tenants' or as 'Tenants In Common', and how you want to split the ownership of the property. For example, you may want to hold the property in the majority of the lower rate tax payer, so that you pay less tax.

Whenever a property is being purchased by more than one person or transferred into multiple ownership your solicitor should always ask you how you wish to hold the property.

STEP 3. Notify HMRC.

If you decide to have an unequal ownership split, then tell HMRC of this split on the Form 17. The Form 17 must be submitted to HMRC within 60 days of the declaration.

Don't delay in notifying HMRC as it could well cost you in tax penalties.

7.7.2. Typical Costs Incurred When Transferring

The costs that you are likely to incur when transferring the property will include the following:

- **Solicitor costs:** These are normally between £300 and £400. However, they will be less than the amount charged when buying a new house as searches will not need to be carried out again.

- **Mortgage lender fees:** The mortgage lender may or may not charge a fee for re-issuing the mortgage in joint names. Try hard to negotiate with them and see if they will waive it.

- **Stamp duty:** This may be payable dependent upon the mortgage amount that is being transferred. For example, if you are transferring more than £125,000 of the mortgage amount to your partner, then stamp duty will be payable at a minimum rate of 1%.

- **A valuation fee may also be incurred, especially if you are using the mortgage re-application** as an opportunity to release some equity from the property.

Please see section 22 to learn more about stamp duty.

It is important that you consider the tax savings you will make before you decide to transfer a property into joint names.

Ideally, you should calculate the cost of transferring the property into joint names and then consider how much income tax you will save on an annual basis.

The case study below demonstrates the importance of making such considerations.

Saving Tax When Moving a Property Into Joint Ownership

Alex has an investment property in his sole name and is a 40% taxpayer.

His wife, Lisa, is unemployed and has no intention of working.

Alex has an outstanding mortgage of £50,000 on the property, which is now worth £100,000.

He gifts 75% of the property to his wife and re-mortgages the property in joint names, with a 75:25 split in favour of his wife.

The cost of transferring into joint ownership is as follows:

- Solicitor costs   £500 approx.
- Mortgage lender fees   £variable
- Stamp duty   N/A. This is because 75% of the £50,000 mortgage is £37,500, and this amount is below the stamp duty threshold value.

He also calculates what the tax savings will be on an annual basis on a property income of £6,000.

| Alex's tax liability | ➔ 40% on £1,500 = £600 | (based on 25% ownership) |
| Lisa's tax liability | ➔ 0% on £4,500 = £0 | (based on 75% ownership) |

By having a 75:25 split, the combined tax liability is £600.

If Alex had kept the property in his sole ownership, then his tax liability would have been £2,400 (40% on £6,000 taxable property income) on an annual basis.

This means that both Alex and Lisa are making an annual income tax savings of £1,800.

8. How To Jointly Own A Property 50:50 But Split Rental Income 90:10!

An article in the *'Times'* stated that 53% of parents plan to financially support their offspring through university. Many will fund via savings, however, there is an alternative method of finance that should be considered.

This alternative method means that parents can subsidise their offspring and still keep their savings intact. There is also an added bonus of a minimal tax bill if correct procedures are followed.

8.1.   What Has To Be Done?

- The parent(s) purchase a property (outright or via a mortgage) which is legally owned jointly with the student.
- The student resides in the property (rent free!) whilst undertaking their studies.
- The property is also let to other students who pay rent to the student as owner.
- The student uses the rent to finance his/her own personal expenditure

8.2.   How Does This Work In Practice?

Many assume that when a property is owned on a joint basis any rental income received is also taxed in accordance with the same percentage proportion of ownership. For example, where a property is owned 50:50 then the assumption is that the rent must be taxed using the same 50:50 proportion.

However, this is not necessarily the case. The rent could be shared in varying proportions calculated to produce the maximum tax advantage for each owner, especially if one owner is a higher rate tax payer and the other a non or basic rate taxpayer.

Example

The purchase deed of 54 Dorchester Place, Oxford, shows that the property is owned jointly by John and his daughter Jane in the proportion 90:10. John is a 45% taxpayer, while Jane is a student and as such is a non-taxpayer. The net rental income for the year is £7,000.

Normally this would mean a tax bill of £2,835 for John on a 90% share of the income taxed at 45% whereas Jane would have no tax liability as the amount allocated to her is 10% i.e. £700 (which is covered by Jane's personal allowance).

On these figures, Jane will have to find another source of income to pay for her university living expenses unless Jack can subsidise her out of his already taxed income. The use of this proportion is therefore neither tax nor cash efficient.

It would therefore be more beneficial for the 90:10 split to be in Jane's favour. This would give Jane an income of £6,300 – below her personal tax limit of £12,500 (2019/20). The balance of £700 would be allocated to John to be taxed at 45% producing a tax bill of just £315.

John would still have £385 (i.e. £700 - £315), which is just enough to pay for any minor property repairs. The result of using this allocation is a tax saving of £2,520 per year and most importantly cash income – tax free - for Jane of £6,300 per year (a massive £18,900 over the three years that she is at university).

8.3. What Does HMRC Think Of This Arrangement?

HMRC do not appear to mind at all! To quote from section 1030 of their 'Property Income Manual' under the heading 'Jointly owned property – no partnership':

"joint owners can agree a different division of profits and losses and so occasionally the share of profits or losses will be different from the share in the property. The share for tax purposes must be the same as actually agreed."

It would, however, be advisable to draw up a formal agreement in case HMRC require confirmation of the allocation. If written correctly, this agreement could accommodate any change in the owners' individual circumstances and the personal allowance amount on an annual basis.

The agreement should preferably be reviewed before the beginning of each tax year to record the allocation to apply for the coming year. An additional point (should HMRC query the allocation) is to ensure that the rental monies are paid in the correct proportions into each individual's bank account, reflecting the agreed share of income.

Importantly, the agreement will have no effect on the allocation of Capital Gains should the property be sold at a later date. Any taxable chargeable gain arising would be divided based on the actual ownership share as per the purchase deed; in the example given above, 90% would be charged to John and 10% to Jane.

8.4. Property Owners Who Are Married Couples

Married couples or civil partners who own property in joint names are automatically taxed using a 50:50 allocation. Therefore, this tax planning exercise only works if the property owners are unmarried. However, married couples can still take advantage of this tax saving scheme by changing the underlying ownership of the property to a different proportion, and using the Form 17 to inform HMRC.

8.5. Getting It Right!

The tax saving plan detailed above is clearly beneficial from an income tax point of view, however, care must be taken when the property is sold. Regardless of how the rental income is treated for income tax purposes it is the underlying beneficial ownership that determines the Capital Gains Tax treatment.

Therefore, the allocation must ensure that the full Capital Gains Tax allowance can be used by each owner. This may not be the case for a married couple who had chosen a 90:10 split, therefore the Declaration would need to be revised preferably a few months prior to the actual sale of the property enabling time for the required changes to be recorded by HMRC.

The plan is only available for adults over the age of 18 as the personal allowance cannot be used against income that comes directly or indirectly from a parent.

If other students shared the property with the owner, a claim for 'Rent a Room' relief could be made for income tax and, so long as the property remained Jane's 'Principal Private Residence', on disposal the property would be exempt from CGT. This would allow the personal allowance to be used against any other income.

Declarations of Trust should be limited to confirmation of the beneficial interest of each owner; any indication as to who should receive the share on death should be stated in a will drawn up by a solicitor.

9. Joint Property And Form 17: Practical Points

It is relatively common for an asset (e.g. an investment property) to be jointly held in the names of a married couple (or civil partners). The general rule is that those individuals are treated for income tax purposes as beneficially entitled to the property income in equal shares. This is sometimes referred to as the '50:50 rule'.

For example, Adam and Brenda are married and living together. Adam is a basic rate taxpayer; Brenda pays tax at the higher rate. They jointly own an investment property (i.e. Adam 75%; Brenda 25%). The property rental income is £10,000. Adam and Brenda each pay tax on income of £5,000.

9.1.   Splitting Income Differently

However, this 50:50 rule is subject to certain exceptions (in ITA 2007, s 836). One important exception is if the individuals make a declaration to HM Revenue and Customs (HMRC) of their unequal beneficial interests (under s 837). This is sometimes called the 'form 17 rule' (i.e. as the declaration is made on form 17). It broadly allows a couple with unequal beneficial interests to be taxed on their actual entitlement to income from jointly held property.

Thus, in the above example, following a valid form 17 declaration, Adam would pay tax (at 20%) on rental income of £7,500, and Brenda would pay tax (at 40%) on £2,500. Their overall income tax bill is therefore lower.

9.2.   Points To Watch

The form 17 process appears straightforward. However, in practice there are various issues and potential problems, some of which are outlined below.

1. Husband and wife (or civil partners) should check that they jointly own the property as 'tenants in common'. A form 17 election cannot be made (i.e. the property income cannot be split other than in equal shares) if the couple own the property as 'joint tenants'.

2. HMRC requires evidence that the couple's beneficial interests are unequal (75:25 in the above example), such as a written declaration or deed.

3. If the property is jointly held in equal shares, it is not possible to make a declaration for income to be divided in unequal shares.

4. The form 17 rule therefore applies if the individuals are beneficially entitled to the income in unequal shares (s 837(1)(a)), such as 60:40, or even 100:0 (see HMRC's Trusts, Settlements and Estates manual at TSEM9848).

5. The declaration on form 17 must be made by both spouses jointly. For example, it cannot be made by one spouse if the other disagrees.

6. The declaration on form 17 must reach HMRC within 60 days from the date of signature of the last spouse to sign; otherwise, it is invalid. HMRC generally enforces this time limit strictly.

7. The form 17 rule only applies to income arising from the date of the declaration (s 837(4)). Thus, a declaration made very late in the tax year may have little or no effect on the couple's overall tax position for that year.

8. HMRC treats a valid declaration on form 17 as continuing to apply in later tax years, until one spouse dies, or the couple separate permanently or divorce, or the beneficial interest of a spouse in the property or income changes (see TSEM9864).

9. Whilst it is not possible for the couple to simply choose to end the split of income resulting from the declaration (unless one of the events in the previous point occurs), it may be possible to stop the declaration on form 17 having effect by making a small change of beneficial interest in the income or property, such as by one spouse transferring part of their beneficial interest to the other (s 837(5)). The 50:50 rule would then apply unless another declaration is made.

9.2.1. Practical Tip

A declaration on form 17 can be useful for income tax purposes. However, there may be other tax implications to consider, depending on the circumstances (e.g. stamp duty land tax), as well as non-tax implications in transferring beneficial interests in property. Professional advice should be sought where necessary.

10. Legal v Beneficial Ownership: A 'Taxing' Distinction!

10.1. Legal And Beneficial Ownership

The two types of ownership are not mutually exclusive, but essentially describe different aspects of property ownership.

While the beneficial owner may often also be the legal owner, (and *vice versa*), this will not always be the case:

- the legal owner is the 'official' or 'formal' owner of the land/property; and
- the beneficial owner is the person with the right to use/occupy the property (without paying for it) and the right to enjoy any income, etc. derived from the property.

A person <u>can</u> be both the legal and beneficial owner of property, at the same time – this is very common.

10.2. Legal Ownership

Legal ownership reflects who is responsible for the land/property. The parties registered under the Land Registry are the legal owners. Under English law, no more than four persons can be formally registered as the legal owners of a parcel of land/property. Those (up to) four persons are essentially equal.

10.3. Beneficial Ownership

The beneficial ownership or 'equitable interest' in property reflects who is entitled to the benefits or fruit of the land, be it in monetary or other form. The law of equity has developed to ensure that fair outcomes are achieved.

Example: Ownership Of A Holiday Home

Bill and Ted put up the funds to buy a holiday home in York. For whatever reason, only Bill's name is noted in the Land Registry. Bill is the legal owner, but Ted is not too bothered by this because he knows that the law of equity will recognise that he is a co-owner and that both Ted and Bill have a beneficial interest in that property.

Furthermore, if Ted put up 2/3rds of the money for the property – i.e. twice Bill's contribution – then the principles of equity will presume that Ted has a greater interest in the property than Bill.

So, if at some future date Bill and Ted's holiday home should be levelled to make way for York's new airport, it will be only equitable to assume that Ted's greater investment at the outset will result in Ted having more of the compensation received.

10.4.   Analogies

One way to look at the distinction between legal and beneficial ownership is to consider a limited company:

- the company has owners – its shareholders. If the company's value increases significantly, so does the value of each shareholder's interest in the company. The shareholders are <u>broadly</u> equivalent to the beneficial owners of land. If the company is sold or liquidated, the shareholders get the proceeds; and
- the company also has official custodians/guardians – principally, its directors. The directors have duties both to the shareholders and to others. If a legal claim is made against the company, it is primarily the directors' responsibility to deal with it on behalf of the shareholders. The company directors are <u>broadly</u> equivalent to the legal owners of land.

It is, of course, very common for directors also to be shareholders – there can be an overlap between the legal responsibility, and the beneficial owners.

Another way to look at the distinction is in terms of trusts. For example, In English law, a child cannot take full legal ownership of land until reaching the age of 18. If a deceased parent's will leaves the family home to a young child, a trustee is appointed to look after the property until the child reaches 18 years old. The trustee(s) will be the legal owner(s), whereas the child is the beneficial owner and:

- he or she may live in it – a right to enjoy or occupy the asset; and
- if the property is rented out instead, the child has the right to any income received; and
- if the property is sold, then the proceeds 'belong' to the child.

10.5.   Tax Implications

Tax is first and foremost about money. It follows that tax is primarily concerned with who has the beneficial interest in the property, in terms of:

(a) who has a right to the income – income tax follows who receives the income (or is entitled to any income arising);

(b) who has a right to the proceeds of any property disposal or part-disposal – capital gains tax (CGT) will be charged on whoever is entitled to the proceeds as beneficial owner; and

(c) who has a right to enjoy or occupy the property – inheritance tax (IHT) will also follow whoever enjoys the use of the asset (see also 'Tax complications' below).

Stamp duty land tax (SDLT) is more complex and that is perhaps understandable, given its origins. It can <u>potentially</u> apply to transfers of either beneficial or legal ownership. This is a complex area, but it is worth noting that SDLT generally applies only where the value of the interest transferred is at least £40,000.

10.6. Tax Complications

10.6.1. Income Tax

While tax generally follows who is entitled to the income, it can also follow who receives the income (albeit generally as a first step).

For example, trustees sometimes have to file tax returns and pay tax on the money they receive on trust assets, even though it will, ultimately, be paid out to the trust's income beneficiaries. But the trustees are effectively paying the tax 'up front' for the income beneficiaries, who get credit on their own tax bills for any tax already paid by the trustees. There can be similar arrangements for non-resident landlords.

10.6.2. Capital Gains Tax

The above example of Bill and Ted is straightforward. But what if Ted says that his investment was only a loan to Bill, so that Bill could actually buy and own the house outright? Or, what if Ted is married, and says that his wife, Gertrude, should also be included for CGT purposes (and use her basic rate band/annual exemption) when the property is sold?

While legal ownership is relatively easy to determine, beneficial ownership can change relatively easily (or be more difficult to pin down in the first place). How the proceeds are divided by the parties is strongly indicative, of course, and HMRC's approach in such cases can be found in its Trusts and Estates manual (at TSEM9900 onwards).

10.6.3. Inheritance Tax

Many readers will be familiar with the 'gifts with reservation of benefit' IHT trap which, says that where a person gives away (for example) the family home, but retains the right to live in it, the home may be deemed never to have left that person's estate for IHT purposes.

This reflects that the original owner may have transferred legal ownership to another party, but has retained an equitable interest – a right to occupy the property – for himself.

10.6.4. Practical Tip

Legal ownership is more concerned with the responsibilities of land ownership, while beneficial ownership is about who benefits from or enjoys the use of the property. Quite rightly, tax usually follows the beneficial owner. But pinning down beneficial ownership can sometimes be problematic, particularly between co-owners and family members. It is worth keeping contemporaneous notes and documentation, in case they are needed later, such as in the event of an HMRC enquiry.

11. Offsetting Interest Charges From 6th April 2017

11.1.   Restricting Tax Relief On Mortgage Interest And Related Finance Costs

IN 2015 the Chancellor announced that tax relief would be restricted for mortgage interest, etc., incurred for the letting of most types of residential property, or "dwelling houses", by individuals.

The restriction was not a complete disallowance but was likely to disadvantage many residential property landlords. In order to soften the blow, the disallowance was being introduced in stages over several tax years – "death by approximately four cuts", if you will.

Once fully implemented, this single measure was expected to cost landlords more than £660million in additional tax.

11.1.1.   Will It Affect Me?

There was more than a good chance that many residential property landlords would be caught by the new rules.

Those who think they will be unaffected because they make only relatively small rental profits should consider carefully the effect of these changes as set out in the **Examples** below.

The new rules affect:
- Finance costs – interest, anything economically equivalent to interest, and incidental costs of obtaining finance, including to
    - Buy a dwelling to let out, or any interest in such a property and even to -
    - Develop land or existing property, to be let out as an ordinary dwelling(s), incurred in relation to -
- "Dwelling houses" – not defined in the legislation but most types of residential accommodation, including its gardens or grounds, by -
- Individuals – which will include individuals acting jointly (see also Partnerships, Companies and Trusts below)

Where the finance costs are incurred only partly for residential letting, then they are to be apportioned on a 'just and reasonable basis'.

When the measure was announced, the government said that it expected that roughly only 20% of individual landlords would be adversely affected.

Given that HMRC also estimates that there are around 1.5million landlords in the UK, even this would represent a very large number.

However, the *real* number of landlords likely to be affected will probably be much higher, since the government appears to have factored in only taxpayers using "Buy-To-Let" ("BTL") mortgages. Most readers will be well aware that there are very many properties which are let out on normal mortgages – or at least not BTL mortgages – for various reasons.

Interest on any loan applied for a Furnished Holiday Letting business are unaffected by the new rules. Hotels are not property businesses from a tax perspective but trades, so will also be unaffected.

11.1.2. Partnerships, Companies And Trusts

The original guidance, which was published, indicated that only individuals would be 'caught' by the new rules. Companies were not mentioned, nor were partnerships. The legislation itself, however, says **that interest will be disallowed for all property businesses subject to Income Tax.**

Individuals, partnerships and Trusts therefore seem all to be caught by the new rules. **Companies are specifically excluded**, except when acting in a fiduciary or representative capacity.

This means that non-Resident Company Landlords will generally escape the new restriction.

However, Trustees should note in particular that the provisions which give Basic Rate tax relief (see below) makes no mention of trusts.

11.1.3. How Will It Affect Me?

In effect, if you are a 40% or 45% taxpayer, then an extra £1 of tax relief from loan interest saves 40p or 45p respectively.

Restricting the tax relief to only 20% – 20p per £1 – means that this measure will effectively cost 20p or 25p in the £1 for Higher and Additional Rate taxpayers respectively.

The restriction will work by disallowing the finance costs entirely in the calculation of taxable rental profits (this part is being phased in over several tax years) and then separately *most** taxpayers will instead be able to claim Basic Rate tax relief of 20% on at least some of their disallowed interest costs. (A partner's share of the rental profits determines his or her share of the tax deduction).

There are, however, various restrictions to the 20% tax credit. This makes the calculation complex but the rationale appears to be that the tax credit is only used against 'full' 20% tax, rather than going against only 7.5% 'new' dividend tax, or savings which might be covered by the new so-called "Allowances" for savings and dividend income.

The adjustments appear to turn a blind eye to losses set against total income, however, which seems quite wasteful.

Most people will concentrate on the loss of Higher / Additional Rate tax relief, but disallowing finance costs and thereby increasing taxable rental income seems likely also to affect people on relatively modest incomes for:

- Student loan repayments
- Tax Credits entitlements

*The Income Tax deduction is available to individuals who are subject to Income Tax on an affected residential rental property business. This may prove problematic for Trusts which make discretionary payments of income to individual beneficiaries.

11.1.4. When Will It Affect Me?

The new rules were phased in from April 2017:

- 2017/18   75% of finance costs allowable as in the past, and 25% gets only 20% tax relief
- 2018/19   50% of finance costs allowable as in the past, and 50% gets only 20% tax relief
- 2019/20   25% of finance costs allowable as in the past, and 75% gets only 20% tax relief
- 2020/21   No finance costs allowed against rental profits, 100% gets a maximum 20% tax relief

11.1.5. Examples Of New Interest Relief Tax Rules

1. Bill is an employed IT programmer and earns £50,000 a year. He is a 40% taxpayer.

He also lets out the property he used to live in, before he moved in with his spouse, and that property generates £5,000 a year net rental income after £3,000 interest deductions on an interest-only mortgage. From 2017/18 the personal allowance has been increased to £11,500, and the basic rate band to £33,500.

Tax Year:	2016/17 £	2017/18 £	2018/19 £	2019/20 £	2020/21 £
Earnings	50,000	50,000	50,000	50,000	50,000
Net Rent after Mortgage	5,000	5,000	5,000	5,000	5,000
Add-back Rental Finance	0	750	1,500	2,250	3,000
Total	55,000	55,750	56,500	57,250	58,000
Tax Liability Original	11,200	11,000	11,300	11,600	11,900
Rental 20% Tax Credit	0	-150	-300	-450	-600
Net Tax	11,200	10,850	11,000	11,150	11,300
Tax increase on 2016/17	0	-320	-200	-50	100

In the end, Bill is paying almost 50% tax on his rental profits, when all of his interest costs have been added back. The disallowance of loan interest relief at his main tax rate costs him far more in tax than the new 20% saving adjustment.

2. James is a full-time property investor, running 15 residential properties. He is heavily geared and his interest repayments eat up about 50% of his rent roll. Let's also assume that his interest costs of £40,000 a year increase by 5% per annum, as rates are expected soon to rise:

	2016/17 £	2017/18 £	2018/19 £	2019/20 £	2020/21 £
Net Rent after Mortgage	40,000	40,000	40,000	40,000	40,000
Add-back Rental Finance	0	10,500	22,050	34,728	48,620
Total	40,000	50,500	62,050	74,728	88,620
Tax Liability					
Original	5,800	8,900	13,520	18,591	24,148
Rental 20% Tax Credit	0	-2,100	-4,410	-6,946	-9,724
Net Tax	5,800	6,800	9,110	11,645	14,424
Tax increase on 2016/17	0	1,000	3,310	5,845	8,624

This example shows why landlords cannot ignore these new rules, even if they currently pay only 20% tax. Critically, the mortgage interest disallowance is enough to make James a 40% Higher Rate taxpayer anyway, because his interest costs are so high.

By 2020/21, James' *taxable* profits are more than double his actual profits because by this point his interest costs are fully disallowed.

11.1.6. What Should I Do?

This might seem like an open invitation to incorporate your property business – and in fact incorporation can offer numerous benefits, depending on the circumstances – but, as many readers will know:

- Companies generally find it harder to secure finance for BTL property
- Interest rates are usually significantly higher for corporate loans
- There may be significant "one-off" costs to incorporating an existing business, such as legal fees, Stamp Duty Land Tax and Capital Gains Tax, although Incorporation Relief may be available, thanks to the **EM Ramsay** case
- In terms of running your own company, dividend income is about to get a lot more expensive (see next Budget development)

If you have both a trade and a residential property business, then it would make sense to ensure that any finance costs are incurred more in respect of the fully deductible trading activity than the residential property business.

Taxpayers and advisers may well want to re-acquaint themselves with the guidance on tax relief on funding capital introduced into a business, in HMRC's Business Income Manual at BIM45700.

A similar approach might benefit those with both commercial and residential properties but 'partitioning' interest costs may be more difficult.

HMRC may well try to argue that, if the rental business is an aggregation for tax purposes, the interest should be apportioned rather than specifically allocated to commercial lettings which escape the disallowance. It is sometimes possible to own property in different capacities so that the net incomes are not aggregated but care and advice will be essential, with an eye in particular to the potential loss of flexibility of rental losses.

Will some landlords ditch residential property completely in favour of commercial letting? I suspect it will increase the appeal of commercials.

12. Offsetting Different Types Of Interest Charges

In this section you will learn about the different types of interest repayments that property investors may come across.

In the earlier case studies below, we will show what can be claimed in the 2017-18 tax year, and also what can be claimed in the 2016-17 too.

However, building on from the previous section, remember:

If the interest was incurred in the 2016-17 tax year, then the entire interest amount can be offset.

If the interest was incurred in the 2017-18 tax year, then 75% of the interest amount can be offset.

12.1.   Interest On Mortgages

It is probably fair to say that this is the most common type of interest that is associated with property investors.

This interest relates to the amount you pay back to your mortgage lender that is above and beyond the initial amount that you borrowed.

> It does not matter if the mortgage is a 'repayment' or an 'interest only' mortgage. The fact that interest repayments have been made means that they can be offset.

This is illustrated through the following case study.

Interest on Mortgages

John buys an investment property for £100,000.

The finance for the property is made up from a £20,000 deposit (provided from his personal savings) and an £80,000 buy-to-let mortgage (provided by a High Street Bank).

In the first year of the mortgage he pays £2,500 in mortgage interest.

Interest incurred in 2016-17 tax year
If the mortgage interest is incurred before 6th April 2017, then this entire amount can be offset against his income from the property.

This means that if he received £5,500 income from his property, he would only be liable to pay tax on £3,000.

Interest incurred in 2017-18 tax year
If the mortgage interest is incurred from 6th April 2017 onwards, then he can

---

offset £1,875 (i.e. 75% of £2,500).

This means that if he received £5,500 income from his property, he would be liable to pay tax on £3,625. He can also knock £625 * 20% = £125 off his final tax bill.

12.2. A Note About 'Interest Only' And 'Repayment Mortgages'

As mentioned in the above tax tip, you are able to claim interest relief regardless of whether you have an 'interest only' mortgage or a 'repayment' mortgage.

12.2.1. Interest Only Mortgage

With an **interest only** mortgage you do actually only pay the interest that is charged on the amount that has been borrowed. The actual amount i.e. the capital amount remains the same and is usually due in one lump sum at the end of the mortgage term.

Interest Only Mortgage

Louise buys a property for £125,000 where her mortgage lender provides £100,000 on an interest only mortgage over 25 years.

Her monthly interest repayment is £500.

At the end of the mortgage term, she will still owe the £100,000 that has been borrowed.

12.2.2. Repayment Mortgage

With a **repayment** mortgage you pay both the interest and the capital amount on a monthly basis. However, you are only able to offset the amount that has been charged in interest. You cannot offset the capital repayments.

Repayment Mortgage

Same scenario as in the previous example. However, this time Louise goes for a repayment mortgage of £100,000.

This means that her monthly repayments will be higher because she is repaying both the interest and part of the capital amount borrowed.

She makes monthly repayments of £650, where £400 is the interest repayment and £250 is capital repayment.

She is only able to offset the interest part of the repayment i.e. the £400. She is not able to offset the capital element of the repayment mortgage.

Interest incurred in 2016-17 tax year
If the £400 mortgage interest is incurred before 6th April 2017, then this entire amount can be offset against his income from the property.

Interest incurred in 2017-18 tax year
If the mortgage interest is incurred from 6th April 2017 onwards, then she can offset £300 (i.e. 75% of £400). She can also reduce her final tax bill by £100 * 20% = £20, per month.

12.3.   Interest On Personal Loans

If you take out a personal loan that is used 'wholly and exclusively' for the purpose of the property, then the interest charged on this loan can also be offset.

The important point to note here is that personal loans *must* be used in connection with the property.

Following are some typical property investment scenarios detailing when the interest charged on a personal loan *can* be offset against the property income.

12.3.1.   Loan Used For Providing Deposit

Most buy-to-let mortgage lenders require you to provide a 20% deposit before they will lend you the remaining 80% in the form of a mortgage.

If you don't have the 20% deposit, then it is likely that you may well need to finance the deposit by getting a personal loan.

If you do take out a personal loan for the 20% deposit, the interest charged on this loan can be offset against the property income.

If you are considering doing this, or have already done this, then what this means is that you have a 100% financed investment property, where interest charged on both the mortgage and the personal loan can be offset against the rental income.

Interest on Personal Loan Used For Deposit

Ali is desperate to buy his first investment property after seeing his pension fund plummet and his house value almost double within 5 years.

Unfortunately, (due to his lavish lifestyle), he has no savings of his own but is in a well-paid job, earning £40,000 per annum.

He sees an investment property advertised for £100,000, but his mortgage lender requests a deposit of £15,000.

He sources this deposit by acquiring a personal loan at a rate of 9% per annum.

The bank then agrees to finance the remaining £85,000.

This means that Ali has a 100% financed investment property. Therefore, he is able to offset interest charged on both his loan and the BTL mortgage against his rental income.

12.3.2. Loan Used For Refurbishments/Developments

Periodically, you will need to refurbish or even develop a property.

Imagine that you have just purchased a property that needs totally re-decorating and modernising. If you take out a loan for this kind of work, then the interest charged on the loan can be offset against the property income.

Alternatively, you might decide to embark on a more expensive property extension, e.g., to build a conservatory.

Again, the same rule applies here: The interest charged on the loan can be offset.

Interest on Personal Loan Used for a Refurbishment

Karen buys an investment property for £100,000. She manages to pay the 15% deposit from her own personal savings and the remaining finance is acquired on a BTL mortgage.

Before letting out the property she decides that a new bathroom suite will greatly increase the chances of the property getting let quickly. She prices a replacement bathroom suite at £2,000.

Unfortunately, she has already stretched her personal savings account by funding the deposit for the property.

Therefore, she applies for, and is successful, in obtaining a £2,000 personal loan at an interest rate of 10%.

Because the personal loan is used to replace the bathroom suite in the investment property she is able to offset the interest charged on the loan against her rental income.

12.3.3.   Loans Used For Purchasing Products

If you purchase goods from retailers where finance is available and these goods are used in your property, then the interest charged can also be offset.

This is more likely to happen if you are providing a fully furnished property, e.g., a luxury apartment.

If this is the case, then you may decide to buy the more expensive items on finance.

Such items are likely to include

- sofas, dining table & chairs, beds;
- cooker, washing machine, fridge/freezer;
- carpets, flooring, etc.

If you are paying for these products over a period of time (e.g., 6, 12, or 18 months), then any interest charged by your creditor can be offset against your rental income.

Interest on Buy-Now-Pay-Later Loans

Continuing from the previous case study.

Once the bathroom suite has been replaced she decides that the property should be offered fully furnished.

She decides to buy some new kitchen furniture in a sale and buys it on a buy-now-pay later scheme where interest is charged at a rate of 27.9%.

Again she is able to offset the interest charged on the loan against the rental income.

12.3.4.   Loans To Continue The Running Of Your Business

There may be occasions when you need to borrow money because your need to pay some bills or employees but do not have sufficient funds in your account.

In such circumstances you may decide to apply for a short-term loan to make these payments. Again the interest charged on the loan can be offset against the property income.

Interest on Loan for Paying Bills & Employees

Alexander has a large portfolio of properties but has incurred a cash flow problem. This is because he has just paid for a major refurbishment on one of his properties by using funds in his property account, rather than acquiring some sort of finance.

This decision means that he is unable to pay his employees (who work in his property business) their end of month salaries and some property related utility bills that are due.

He applies for a short-term loan of £5,000 to make the necessary payments and interest is charged at 8%.

His is able to offset the interest charged against the income from his properties because it is incurred for the purpose of his property business.

12.3.5. Interest On Overdrafts

If you have a separate bank account set-up for your property investment business then you may decide to apply for an overdraft rather than a personal loan.

If you decide to do this then as long as the overdraft is used for the purpose of the property business, then you can offset the interest charged on the overdraft.

Interest Charged on Overdrafts

Using the previous example.

Instead of applying for a loan, Alexander decides to request a one-year overdraft limit on his account of £5,000. His application is successful and he is charged an interest rate of 7.5%.

Whenever he uses his overdraft facility and interest is charged, he is able to offset it against his rental income.

12.4. Interest On Re-Mortgages

If you have a mortgage on your investment property, then it is highly likely that you will consider moving to another lender at some point.

The main reason for this is because you will be trying hard to find a better mortgage deal!

As interest rates have been falling over the past few years, more and more people have been re-mortgaging their investment properties to capitalise on the better deals and to help grow their property portfolios.

Below are some pointers about re-mortgaging.

a) If you re-mortgage your outstanding mortgage with another lender, then you can *still* offset the interest repayments.

Interest on Re-Mortgages

Timothy has an outstanding mortgage balance of £50,000 on his investment property. He decides to move his mortgage from the Nat West to Lloyds as they are offering a lower rate of interest.

Timothy can still offset interest charged by Lloyds on the £50,000 re-mortgage.

b) If you re-mortgage for a lower amount, then you can still offset the whole mortgage interest.

Re-mortgaging for a Different Value

Imagine the same scenario as in the previous example, where Timothy has an outstanding balance of £50,000 on his investment mortgage.

However, he inherits £20,000 from a family member, so he decides to use this toward lowering his mortgage liability.

Therefore, he only re-mortgages to the value of £30,000 with Lloyds.

Again, the interest charged on the £30,000 can be offset against the property income.

c) If you re-mortgage for a greater amount, then generally speaking you can only offset the additional amount if it is used for the purpose of an investment property (however you may be able to exploit paragraph BIM45700).

As property prices have sharply risen over the past few years, investors have been re-mortgaging their properties for higher values.

This is known as **releasing equity.**

If you have released equity or are considering doing this, then you need to follow the guidelines given above regarding the interest charged on personal loans.

You need to ask yourself,

'Is the additional equity release being used for the sole purpose of my property business?'

This can be illustrated through the following case study.

Releasing Equity

Timothy has an outstanding balance of £50,000 on his investment mortgage.

However, his property value has appreciated considerably, so he decides to re-mortgage with Lloyds for £80,000.

This means that he is releasing additional equity out of his current property to the value of £30,000.

He decides to use the equity release in the following way:

£20,000 is used to fund a new property investment, and it provides the deposit for his next buy-to-let investment. £10,000 is used to pay for a new car for his wife.

Now, Timothy can *only* offset the interest charged on both the outstanding mortgage balance of £50,000 and the £20,000 he is using as a deposit for his next purchase.

This is because this combined amount of £70,000 is used 'wholly and exclusively' for his property investments.

However, he *cannot* use the interest charged on £10,000 for buying the car as this cost is not associated with his property investments.

d) Generally speaking, because it is possible to obtain a lower rate of interest on your residential mortgage, more and more investors are deciding to increase the borrowing on their main residence and using this to reduce the investment mortgages.

Releasing Equity from Main Residence

Jack and Louise have a residential mortgage on their private residence for £100,000. The interest rate is fixed at 4.5%. They also have a BTL investment property. The outstanding mortgage on this property is also £100,000 but the interest rate is at a higher rate of 6.5%.

Because their main residence has a value of £300,000, they release £100,000 equity from their main residence, at the same rate of 4.5%, and pay off the outstanding debt of £100,000 on the investment property.

Again the interest charged on the £100,000 equity release can be offset against the rental income off the investment property.

13. 'Wholly And Exclusively'

This section will address the term 'wholly and exclusively.'

If you have ever read and tried to digest the <u>Property Income</u> Manual, then you will have noticed that this phrase is consistently mentioned in the guide.

By the time you have finished this section, you will know how to test if an expense satisfies this rule and whether it can be offset against your property rental income.

13.1. Understanding The Term 'Wholly And Exclusively'

> HMRC state,
>
> **'You can't deduct expenses unless they are incurred wholly and exclusively for business purposes.'**

To put it simply, this statement means that if you incurred an expense that was not used for the purpose of your property, in any way at all, then you cannot offset the cost.

Whenever you incur a cost for your investment property, always ask yourself,

'Has the cost been incurred wholly and exclusively for the property?'

If you can answer **YES** to this question, then it is highly likely you will be able to offset the cost against your property rental income.

13.2. What If Cost Is Not Wholly And Exclusively Incurred For Property?

Sometimes you may incur a cost that is not used 'wholly and exclusively' for your property. However, a portion of the cost has been incurred for your property.

For such situations HMRC provide the following guideline:

'Where a definite part or proportion of an expense is wholly and exclusively incurred for the purposes of the business, you can deduct that part or proportion.'

What this effectively means is that you need to determine what part or proportion of the cost is attributed to your investment property. This is because you cannot offset the entire cost.

The following case study will help to illustrate this guideline.

Where Costs Are Not Wholly and Exclusively Incurred for Property

Bill has an investment property.

The bathroom is looking rather 'tired,' so he decides to re-tile it completely. He goes to a local tile shop, where they have an offer of 12 square metres of tiles for £240.

However, he only requires seven square metres for his investment property.

After some serious head scratching he appreciates that the deal is an excellent value for the money and too good to miss. He therefore purchases the tiles.

He decides to use the extra 5 square metres of tiles in his own house.

This means that the entire cost has not been incurred wholly and exclusively for the property. However, a portion of the cost, i.e., 7/12ths, has been incurred wholly and exclusively for the property.

He may therefore offset £140 (i.e., 7/12ths of £240) against his rental income.

13.3. Costs Of Maintenance And Repairs

Once you have purchased and successfully let your property, any maintenance costs incurred that help prevent the property from deteriorating can be offset against your rental income.

It is very likely that at some point you will have to carry out some maintenance work to keep your property in an acceptable state of repair.

When this happens, you will be able to offset the cost against your property income as long as it satisfies the following condition.

- **It is not a capital improvement.**
  A capital improvement is when work is carried out that increases the value of the property.

> **Maintenance Cost**
>
> John is informed by his tenants that water is leaking from the upstairs bathroom into the downstairs living room.
>
> He calls a plumber to repair the damaged bathroom water pipe and also hires a painter/decorator to redecorate the damaged ceiling.
>
> The entire cost of the work is £300, and it can be offset against the rental income.

13.4. Typical Maintenance/Repair Costs

The following list details typical maintenance/repair costs that you are likely to incur and which you can offset against your rental income:

- repairing water/gas leaks, burst pipes, etc.;
- repairing electrical faults;
- fixing broken windows, doors, gutters, roof slates/tiles, etc.;
- repairing internal/external walls, roofs, floors, etc.;
- painting and redecorating the property;
- treating damp/rot;
- re-pointing, stone cleaning, etc.;
- hiring equipment to carry out necessary repair work;
- repairing existing fixtures and fittings which include:
  - radiators,
  - boilers,
  - water tanks,
  - bathroom suites,
  - electrical/gas appliances,
  - furniture, and furnishings, etc.

13.5. The Big Misconception About Costs When A Property Is First Let?

There is a common misconception among buy to let landlords – and some of their accountants – that the cost of repairs to a newly-purchased property cannot be claimed before it is first let out.

13.5.1. Allowable Expenses

In fact, such repairs are an allowable expense provided certain conditions are met, and if allowable, they are treated as if they were incurred on the first day the property is occupied.

The important distinction is between work on the property which is "capital expenditure" - effectively, part of the cost of acquiring the property and making it fit for use in the letting business, and expenditure which is no more than routine maintenance – even if that maintenance is quite extensive as a result of the previous owner's neglect.

13.5.2. The Test

The test is this: was the property fit to be let before the repairs were carried out? If it was, then the repairs are an allowable expense against the rent once the property is let.

The law on this subject is derived from two tax cases which were heard shortly after the end of the Second World War.

13.5.3. A Cinema

In one case, Odeon Cinemas claimed the cost of repairs to various cinemas they had bought up after the end of the war and refurbished before opening them to the public again.

Although the cinemas in question were in a poor state of repair, the Court was satisfied that they were nevertheless usable, and Odeon were simply carrying out routine maintenance which had been neglected during the war. They were also satisfied that the price Odeon paid for the cinemas was not significantly lower as a result of the condition they were in.

13.5.4. A Ship

The other case concerned a ship which was also bought just after the end of the war. It too was in a poor state of repair, to the extent that it was classified as not being seaworthy. Given the times, a temporary certificate of seaworthiness was granted on condition that the ship was sailed straight to a port where it could be extensively repaired.

When the claim for these repairs came to court, the verdict went against the ship-owners. This was because it was clear that (despite the temporary certificate granted because of the post-war shortage of ships) the ship was not fit for use and the repairs were necessary before it could be used for the owner's trade.

It was also the case that the price paid for the ship reflected the fact that it was unseaworthy. The cost of the repairs was therefore capital expenditure, being part of the cost of acquiring the ship as a useable asset for the trade, in contrast to the Odeon cinemas, which were already useable when purchased, and simply needed their neglected routine maintenance brought up to date.

13.5.5. Is Your Property A Cinema Or A Ship?

This distinction between capital expenditure and repairs applies to any work carried out on a property, at any stage in its ownership, and there is nothing special about work carried out before the first letting. The same rules apply, and expenditure on normal maintenance is an allowable expense whether the property has already been let or it has only just been purchased.

That is why a landlord should look at the property he has just bought for his letting business and consider whether it is more like a rather tatty cinema, or an unseaworthy ship!

If you have difficulty persuading your accountant that this is the correct view, tell him to go to HM Revenue and Customs' website, and look at PIM2030 in their Property Income Manual under "Repairs etc. after a property is acquired".

13.6.   Capital Improvements

If you carry out a capital improvement, then you *cannot* offset this cost against your rental income.

This is because it is not classed as maintenance or repair work.

Capital Improvements

After years of owning his investment property, Fred applies for, and gets approval to add, a conservatory.

The cost of the conservatory is £20,000.

Because the conservatory has increased the value of the house by £30,000, it cannot be offset against the rental income.

Again, the cost will be offset against any capital gain that he makes when he sells the property.

REMEMBER: If you have made a capital improvement, then this cost can be claimed when you sell your property.

14. Replacing Your Fixtures And Fittings

This section will help you to understand what is meant by the term **fixtures and fittings** and when you can offset the replacement of them against your income tax.

14.1.   What Are Fixtures And Fittings?

These are items that are classed as being an integral part of the property. If a new tenant moves into a property, then they will expect these items to be in the property.

Examples of fixtures and fittings include

- windows, doors, light fittings;
- kitchen units;
- bathroom suites;
- gas central heating systems and radiators or hot water supply tanks;
- gas fires, etc.

The most important point to understand about fixtures and fittings is that any cost incurred in repairing them or replacing them with a like-for-like product can be offset against the property rental income. This is regardless of whether the property is un-furnished, partly furnished, or fully furnished.

For the remainder of this section we will focus on the replacement of fixtures and fittings.

Two important conditions must be satisfied before you can offset the cost of replacing fixtures and fittings. These are the following.

   a) The cost must be a 'replacement' cost. In other words, it cannot be for the installation of fixtures and fittings that were not previously in the property.

   b) The cost must be for a similar, like-for-like product.

If both these conditions are met, then the cost can be deducted from the rental profits.

14.2.   Replacing Fixtures And Fittings

Whenever you decide to replace existing fixtures and fittings, they are likely to fall into one of the following three categories:

   a) like-for-like replacement;
   b) like-for-like replacement but with capital improvements;
   c) replacement with superior fixtures and fittings.

Each of the above scenarios is treated differently when it comes to calculating your income tax bill, and each is illustrated in the following sections.

14.2.1. Like-For-Like Replacement

If you replace existing fixtures and fittings with similar like-for-like products, then the entire cost can be offset against the income tax bill.

Replacing With Like-for-Like (1)

Alex has been renting out his buy-to-let property for seven years and decides that it is now time to change the bathroom suite.

He finds a similar bathroom suite of comparable quality that costs £500. The cost of having the old suite removed and the new one fitted is also £500.

This means that the entire project costs £1,000.

This whole amount can be offset against the annual rental income.

14.2.2. What If It Is Not Possible To Replace With Like-For-Like?

HMRC appreciate that it is not possible to replace with a like-for-like product in all instances. This is especially true if you are replacing something that is several years old as a like-for-like product may no longer be available.

In such circumstances, it is possible to replace with a superior item, especially if it is of a similar cost.

Replacing With Like-for-Like (2)

Alex also decides to replace the wooden, single-glazed windows as they are starting to rot. The windows are more than 10 years old.

The cost of replacing with similar single-glazed windows is £3,500, and this includes the fitting and removal of the old, rotten windows.

However, the cost of replacing the windows with UPVC double-glazed windows is cheaper and costs £3,400. This price also includes the fitting and removal of the old windows.

Although the UPVC double-glazed windows are of a superior quality, HMRC accept that these types of windows are the 'standard' in all new build properties.

Therefore, it is possible to use these as replacements and offset the entire cost incurred.

14.2.3. Like-For-Like Replacement But With Capital Improvements

If you replace the existing fixtures and fittings with a like-for-like product but also make a capital improvement, then you can only offset the cost of the like-for-like replacement.

Replacing With Like-for-Like but with Capital Improvement

Alex also decides to replace the kitchen units.

The cost of replacing the kitchen units with like-for-like replacements is £1,600. However, he has some additional space that he wishes to utilise, so he orders an additional three units at a cost of £600.

Alex is able to offset the cost of the £1,600 like-for-like replacement against his rental income.

However, the additional three units are treated as a capital improvement, and this cost cannot be offset against the rental income.

Instead, the cost of the additional units can be offset against any capital gain arising when the property is sold.

14.2.4. Replacement With Superior Fixture And Fittings

If you replace the existing fixtures and fittings with superior fixture and fittings, then it will be treated as a capital improvement.

15. Other Ways To Reduce Your Income Tax Bill

In the strategies to date you have learned about the common costs that can be offset against the rental income.

In this section you will now become familiar with numerous other typical costs that a property investor is likely to incur and that can be offset against the rental income.

15.1. Rents, Rates, And Insurance

The following costs are incurred by property investors when the property is let or when the property is empty and between lets.

15.1.1. Rents

The most common type of rent that an investor is likely to incur is ground rent. Landlords are liable to pay this rent on any leasehold property/land, and therefore any such expenditure can be offset against the rental income.

15.1.2. Rates

If you decide to pay any of the following rates on your property, then they can be offset against the rental income:

- water;
- electricity;
- gas;
- council tax;
- service charges;
- TV licence;
- telephone line rental;
- satellite TV charges, etc.

15.1.3. Insurance

Any insurance premiums that you pay for your properties or products/services relating to your property can also be offset against the rental income.

The most common premiums you are likely to pay will include the following:

- building insurance;
- contents insurance;
- insurance cover for service supplies such as
  - gas central heating,
  - plumbing insurance,
  - electrical insurance;
- insurance cover for appliances such as
  - washer/dryer,
  - fridge/freezer,
  - television, etc.

15.2. Can I Offset Pre-Trading Expenditure?

This is a bit of a grey area as far as taxation goes.

The rules for pre-trading expenditure are quite complex, but in theory you can claim expenses incurred in the seven years before commencement of the rental 'business.

The expenses are treated as incurred on the first day the rental 'business' starts.

Having said that, HMRC will want to examine these expenses closely with a view to establishing whether they were incurred 'wholly and exclusively' for the purposes of the 'trade.'

Again in theory HMRC can disallow any expense which has a duality of purpose, but in practice they will usually allow a split to be made.

They will also examine the expenses to see whether they are capital or revenue in nature.

Below is a list of some common types of pre-trading expenditure you are likely to incur before you buy your property:

- travel costs
- the cost of purchasing dedicated trade/magazines for helping you to find your property;
- the cost of telephone calls when phoning estate agents/property vendors, etc.

The important point to note is that each occurrence of a pre-trading expenditure must be incurred wholly and exclusively for the property.

15.3. Carrying Over Rental Losses

> Any rental losses made on a property can be carried forward into the next financial year.

Sometimes you will incur a rental loss on your property investment. Rental losses can be incurred intentionally or unintentionally. The important point to note is that any losses can be carried forward into the next year and can be used to reduce your tax liability for that year.

Carrying Over Rental Losses

After three years of owning his two-bedroom buy-to-let property, John decides to replace the bathroom suite. The cost of replacing it with a like-for-like replacement is £2,500.

His rental income for the property is £4,800 annually, but after all his annual expenses are deducted, e.g., offsetting interest payments, the cost of the replacement bathroom suite, etc., he is left with a £1,000 rental loss.

This loss can be carried forward and offset against his rental income the following year.

15.4.   Claiming Travel Costs

Below is an explanation of travel costs by Jennifer Adams.

A rented property portfolio may not be placed in the same street or even the same town as your main residence or place of work. Travel from one property to another, as the landlord dealing with problems as they arise, does cost. That cost is allowed as an expense against rental income received.

The treatment of travel expenses is similar to that as incurred by a trade or profession, such that to be allowed two key conditions need to be met:

- The expense must be related to the property in that it satisfies the *'wholly and exclusively'* test; and

- It must not be incurred as a capital improvement such that the value of the property is increased.

15.4.1.   *'Wholly And Exclusively'*

Confirmation that profits of a property are calculated using the same rules as for the computation of trading income is to be found in the tax legislation at s 272 of the *Income Tax (Trading and Other Income Act) 2005* (ITTOIA 2005) and hence the *'wholly and exclusively'* rule applies such that there must not be duality of purpose of the expense incurred.

15.4.2.   Office Based At Home

It is a question of fact as to whether the landlord carries on the rental business from his home. If so, the cost of all trips from home (e.g. to check on the investment property/liaise with tenants etc.) are fully allowable, provided that the visit is not also combined with a personal reason.

However, a deduction would still be possible for a journey where any personal benefit is incidental (i.e. *'de minimis'*); for example, the trip is made to the rental property, but the landlord stops on the way to pick up a newspaper.

Furthermore, when making a claim for travelling expenses between the home base and a let property the real reason for the trip may need to be considered carefully.

For example, a landlord lets his main residence in Woking whilst working away from home in Brighton. He has travelled to Woking with his family to visit relatives at Christmas. Whilst in the area he may decide to drop by the rented property for a visit - this will be deemed a 'duality of purpose' visit, not fulfilling the 'wholly and exclusively' rules and hence the cost of travel will be disallowed for tax purposes.

Similarly, if the owner lives in London and has both a holiday home and a letting property based a few miles away from each other in Dorset, the cost of travel would only be allowed if the trip was made straight from the London base to the letting property without stopping at the holiday home first.

However, it would be fair to claim mileage from the holiday home to the let property.

15.4.3. Office Outside Of Home

If the property business is *managed* from an office outside of the home then HMRC deems the business not to be carried on at home, even if the property owner sometimes works from home. In this situation the cost of journeys between home and either the property let or that office base will not be allowable.

However, the cost of travel from the office to and from the properties, and also between properties, will be allowable provided that the trip is incurred '*wholly and exclusively*' for rental business purposes.

15.4.4. Use Of A Letting Agent

Some landlords engage a letting agent to manage the collection of rents, organise services etc. Where such an agent carries out all (or virtually all) the duties relating to the letting activity, it is likely that the rental business is being conducted through the agent.

In such circumstances, the business 'base' is deemed to be the agent's office and as such travelling expenses from the landlords' home to the property are not allowable but will be from the agents office to the property.

15.4.5. Relevant Tax Cases

Under the tax legislation (ITTOIA 2005, s 272) these cases are now relevant to a rental business:

- **Newsom v Robertson [1952]** - a barrister frequently worked from home but his chambers were separate. As such he was deemed not to be carrying on his profession from home and travel between home and chambers was not *wholly and exclusively* incurred for the purposes of his profession.

- **Horton v Young [1971]** - it was found that the claimant did carry on his trade from home and as such travel from home to the various sites at which he worked was undertaken for the purposes of the trade and claimable.

15.4.6. How Much To Claim?

- **Capital expenditure**

If the landlord uses his own car for travel, the full capital purchase cost of the car is not allowable; rather a proportion is, as capital allowances, claimed in the proportion of business use.

The '*wholly and exclusively*' rule also applies to that amount claimed and as with car running expenses only the business proportion is allowed. For detailed guidance see https://www.gov.uk/hmrc-internal-manuals/property-income-manual/pim2220 and PIM3010 onwards, and HMRC's Capital Allowances manual.

- **Running expenses**

There are two methods of calculation for car expenses incurred - the same as for other business expenses.

1. A fixed rate for each mile travelled on business using HMRC's fixed mileage rates. Currently the first 10,000 business miles in relation to the rental business are claimed at 45p and 25p thereafter. This method of calculation is only available where certain conditions are met.

2. On an actual basis, such that the actual expenses (fuel, repairs, insurance etc.) are totalled and apportioned between business and private percentage using detailed records. For example, if a landlord agrees with HMRC that 70% of mileage incurred relates to expenses for the property business a 70% deduction is claimed (the same percentage is used for the capital allowance claim). Provided that the landlord proposes a percentage to add back/disallow which reasonably reflects the private element, HMRC will usually accept.

15.4.7. Misc. Travel Costs

If the trip to visit the property requires an overnight stay, then hotel costs and meals in restaurants can be claimed; if public transport is used then the claim is the cost of the ticket.

15.4.8. Foreign Travel

- If a foreign property is rented out then similar to any other business travel costs, car parking, hotel expenses, petrol, toll charges, flight costs etc. can be claimed providing that you can prove no 'duality of purpose' (e.g. that you did not visit the property whilst also on holiday)
- Incidentally, all foreign property rentals are treated as one business. Hence a claim can be made for the cost of travel to Dubai to look for a possible new rental property against the rental income from a villa already owned in Spain.

15.4.9. Expenses When Not Available For Letting

Expenses incurred during any period whilst the property is *'not available for letting'*, are not deductible for tax purposes. This not only means that travel costs cannot be claimed but it also results in restrictions being made on other expenses that would otherwise be claimed including the mortgage interest.

15.5. General Property Costs

If you have a portfolio and incur expenses then it may not be possible to attribute the cost to a single property. This is because the expenditure may have been for all of the properties.

A good example of this is when purchasing decorating materials for a property. In such circumstances you can either:

- apportion the cost against the properties, or
- have a separate listing of generic expenses to add on at the end when you combine all the incomes and expenditures.

Either way is fine, as it makes no difference to the tax position, though practically the latter option may be easier and simpler to implement.

15.6.   Storage Costs

A cost incurred by an increasing number of investors is storage costs.

The cost of renting storage space is allowable against rental income. The reason is that it fulfils the principal criteria of "wholly and exclusively", as the cost was incurred for the purpose of your property business. If you never had rented property then you would not be incurring such costs.

Storage Costs

John owns 5 properties which are all fully furnished. However, he finds a new long-term tenant for his property who has his own furniture and furnishings. John decides that he will empty the property and store the furniture in rented storage. The cost of rental storage is £450. This amount can be offset against the rental income as it has been incurred 'wholly and exclusively' for the purpose of the rental business.

15.7.   Other Common Landlord Expenditures

Below is a list of other common costs that a landlord will incur that can be offset against the rental income:

- safety certificates, e.g., gas and electrical safety;
- stationery, e.g., stamps, envelopes, books;
- computer equipment;
- bad debts;
- legal and professional costs, e.g., accountancy costs;
- service costs, e.g., window cleaner, gardener;
- furniture/appliance rentals;
- advertisement costs;
- letting agent costs;
- books, magazines, etc.;
- security/smoke alarms;
- telephone calls, including mobile telephone bills (but make sure you have an itemised bill to prove the calls made);
- bank charges (e.g., interest charged on property bank account).

15.8.   Can I Offset The Cost Of A Property Seminar?

During the property investment boom a large number of potential and inexperienced investors attended seminars and paid thousands of pounds for learning about various property investment techniques.

A common question that arises is whether the cost of the seminar can be offset against any future income tax bill.

When asked the question **'Can I offset the cost of a £5,000 property seminar?'** Arthur Weller provides the following guidance:

If the cost of the seminar is wholly and exclusively for the purposes of the trade presently carried out by the taxpayer, then it is allowable.

Here is what HMRC have to say about the matter:

> *'Expenditure on training courses attended by the proprietor of a business with the purpose of up-dating his or her skills and professional expertise is normally revenue expenditure, which is deductible from profits of the business provided it is incurred wholly and exclusively for the purposes of the trade or profession carried on by the individual at the time the training is undertaken'.*

So what exactly does that mean?

Already a property investor
If you are already a property investor, with a portfolio, and attend the course to update your investment skills, then you can offset the entire cost.

You can offset the cost as you will be regarded as updating your skills.

When You CAN Offset the Cost of a £5,000 Property Course

Bill has been investing in property since the early 1980s and has built a portfolio of 12 properties.

However, in 1999 he decides take property investment more seriously and attends a £5,000 course to update and sharpen his investment skills so that he can focus on emerging areas for investment.

The entire cost of the course can be offset against his rental income.

New to property investment
However, if you want to start investing in property and attend a course to learn how to do this, then you will not be able to offset the costs against the rental income.

You cannot offset the cost as you will not be 'updating' your skills in your current profession.

> **When You CANNOT Offset the Cost of a £5,000 Property Course**
>
> Following the collapse of the stock market, John decides that the only way he will be able to maintain his lifestyle when he retires is if he invests in property.
>
> So, in 2001 he attends a property investment course to learn all about property investment. Shortly after the course he buys his first investment property. The cost of the course cannot be offset against any future rental income.

A word of warning
If you do decide to make a claim, it could well trigger an investigation. HMRC do keep a close eye on large amounts being claimed, so be warned!

15.9.   Capital Allowances For Landlords

If you decide to purchase a piece of equipment or an asset that is used for the purpose of the business, then you can claim an 18% annual depreciation allowance. Examples of such assets include:

- Computers and office furniture (that you use in your own home for running the business)
- Tools for maintaining upkeep of properties i.e. DIY tools
- Vehicles (please note that there are new rules for claiming capital allowances on vehicles for expenditure incurred from April 09 onwards).

The depreciation allowance can be claimed annually until the equipment/asset is disposed of. Here is an example that shows how the 18% depreciation allowance works.

> **Capital Allowances for Assets**
>
> Wasim has a portfolio of five investment properties. He also carries out much of the maintenance and repairs on the properties himself, so he decides to purchase professional DIY toolkit for £150 in April 2012. The annual depreciation allowance is calculated as follows:
>
> | Tax Year | Toolkit Value | Annual Rate | Annual Allowance |
> |---|---|---|---|
> | 2015-2016 | £150 | 18% | £27 |
> | 2016-2017 | £123 | 18% | £22 |
> | 2017-2018 | £101 | 18% | £18 |
> | 2018-2019 | £83 | 18% | £15 |
> | 2019-2020 | £68 | 18% | £12 |
>
> As you can see from the above example, the amount that can be claimed on an annual basis continues to decrease as the toolkit value decreases.

16. Running Your Property Business From Home

Many small businesses are run from home and a proportion of the costs of running and maintaining the home can be deducted in computing the profits of the business.

Broadly speaking, expenses fall into two categories – fixed costs and running costs. Fixed costs are those that have to be incurred regardless of the level of trade. Costs that relate to the house as a whole will generally fall into this category. Running costs (or variable costs) are costs that vary depending on the extent of use, such as electricity.

This strategy looks at how relief may be obtained for the fixed cost and at example of typical fixed costs in respect of which relief may be available.

16.1.   Nature Of Relief

Where a business is run from home and part of the home is set aside solely for business use for a specific period, a proportion of the fixed costs incurred in relation to the home will be allowed as a deduction in computing the business profits. It will generally be necessary to apportion the fixed costs between the business and non-business element. A reasonable basis of apportionment would be one which reflects the proportion of the house used for solely business purposes and the time for which it is so used.

Using an area of the house solely for business purposes can have capital gains tax consequences, as the main residence exemption does not apply to any part of the property used for business use. Where only a small part of the house is used solely for business, in most cases the availability of the annual exemption means this is rarely a problem in practice, as any chargeable gain arising is normally covered by the annual exemption. However, to be on the safe side it is sensible to set aside the room used for the business for sole business use during working hours to preserve the deduction for fixed costs but to make it available to the family in evenings and at weekends to keep it within the main residence exemption.

16.2.   Typical Fixed Costs

Costs which may be incurred in relation to a house or other property and which are classified as fixed costs include:

- buildings and contents insurance;
- council tax;
- mortgage interest;
- rent; and
- repairs and maintenance.

Each of these is discussed in more detail below.

16.3.   Insurance

Depending on the nature of the policy, insurance can be either a fixed or a variable cost. Buildings insurance will generally cover the whole property, and where a business is operated from home a deduction can be obtained for a proportion of the premium.

As regards contents insurance, if contents are covered as part of a general buildings and contents policy, a proportion of the total premium can be deducted; likewise, in relation to a separate contents policy that covers all household contents and does not exclude business items. However, if there is a specific trade policy, the premiums for that will be deductible in full, but there will be no deduction in relation to the domestic policy.

16.4.   Council Tax

The extent to which a deduction is permitted in respect of council tax will depend on the circumstances. Council tax is a property-based tax payable on chargeable dwellings. By contrast, business rates are charged on commercial property. Depending on the size and scale of the business and the degree to which the premises are used for business purposes, the council may charge business rates.

However, where a trader merely sets aside a room in his or her home as an office, it is likely that only a council tax charge will apply. Where this is the case, the trader can claim a proportion of the council tax as a deduction in computing the profits of his or her business.

16.5.   Mortgage Costs

Where the house is subject to a mortgage, a deduction may be permissible in respect of a portion of the mortgage costs. However, where the mortgage is a repayment mortgage it is necessary to split the payments into the capital repayment element and the interest element. Repayments of capital are not deductible, whereas a deduction is allowed in respect of the interest element and the trader can claim a portion of the interest element of a mortgage as a deduction in computing profits.

16.6.   Rent

Where the trader rents his or her home and runs a business from a home office, a deduction is also available in computing profit if part of the home is used solely for business purposes. The allowable amount is the proportion of the rent payable to the landlord that is attributable to that part of the home used solely for business purposes.

It should be noted that where the business is run as a limited company, the homeowner can charge rent to his or her company in respect of the part of the home used by the company. The rent paid is deductible by the company in computing the profits for corporation tax purposes, and the homeowner is taxed on the rent that he or she receives. By contrast, where the business is operated by a sole trader, the homeowner cannot charge the business rent.

16.7.   Repairs And Maintenance

All buildings will need some general maintenance at some point. Where part of the home is used solely for business purposes, a deduction is permitted for a proportion of general household repairs and maintenance to the extent that they apply to the property generally, rather than to a specific room.

Examples of repairs and maintenance costs which may be apportioned include roof repairs and painting the exterior of a property. However, where the repairs or maintenance relate solely to a part of the room which is not used for business purposes, no deduction is permitted. By contrast, repairs or maintenance that relate wholly to the part that is used for business purposes are deductible in full.

It should be noted that no relief is available in respect of capital expenditure and a distinction is drawn between a repair (for which a deduction may be allowed) and improvements which are capital in nature and not deductible in computing profits. As a general rule, a repair restores something to its original condition, whereas an improvement significantly enhances it.

16.7.1. Practical Tip

It is easy to overlook the fixed costs of running a home when computing business profits, but it can be worthwhile claiming a deduction where part of the home is used exclusively for business. An additional deduction is available for running costs, which can be claimed either by reference to the actual costs incurred or by using the statutory simplified expenses deduction.

17. Tenant Deposits: Traps & Tips

17.1. Deposits From Tenants

It is common practice for a landlord to take a deposit from a tenant when letting a property to cover the cost of any damage caused to the property by the tenant. A deposit of this nature may be referred to as a security deposit, a damage deposit or a rental deposit. The landlord may also ask for a holding deposit in return for taking the property off the market while the necessary paperwork is undertaken.

17.2. Security Deposits

It is normal practice for landlords to take a security deposit from tenants when letting residential property. The purpose of the deposit is to cover items such as damage to the property that extends beyond normal wear and tear, the cost of having the property, including the carpets, professionally cleaned, removing any rubbish from the property, unpaid rent and such like. The items covered by the security deposit should be stated in the letting agreement.

The deposit charged can be up to two months' rent, although in practice six weeks' rent is common.

Deposits taken by a landlord or agent for an assured shorthold tenancy in England or Wales are protected by Government authorised schemes. There are three possible schemes:

- the Deposit Protection Service scheme;
- the Tenancy Deposits Solution scheme; and
- The Dispute Service scheme.

To remove the need to go to court to settle disputes over retention and repayment of the deposit, each scheme features an alternative dispute resolution service. In the event that there is a dispute regarding the repayment of the deposit in the case of damage or unpaid rent, the alternative dispute resolution service will arbitrate.

The burden of proof falls on the landlord or agent, who will need to provide evidence to support their claim that all or part of the deposit should be retained. If there is no dispute, the tenant's deposit should be returned to the tenant at the end of the tenancy.

The extent to which the deposit is included as income of the rental business depends on whether all or part of the deposit is retained by the landlord. In a straightforward case where a security deposit is taken by the landlord, held for the period of the tenancy and returned to the tenant at the end of the rental period, the deposit is not included as income of the property rental business.

However, if at the end of the tenancy agreement the landlord retains all or part of the deposit to cover damage to the property, cleaning costs or other similar expenses, the amount retained is included as income of the property rental business.

The retained deposit is a receipt of the business in the same way as rent received from the tenant. However, the actual costs incurred by the landlord in making good the damage or having the property professionally cleaned are deducted in computing the profits of the business.

The retained deposit is reflected as rental income of the property rental business for the period in which the decision to retain the deposit is taken, rather than for the period in which the deposit was initially collected from the tenant.

Example
Bill purchases a property as a buy to let investment. He lets the property out in September 2009. He collects a security deposit of £1,000 from the tenant. The terms of the deposit are set out in the tenancy agreement.

The let comes to an end in September 2011. When checking out the tenant, it transpires that the tenant has failed to have the carpets professionally cleaned, as per the terms of the agreement, and also that he has damaged a door, which needs to be repaired.

After discussion, Bill and the tenant agree that Bill will retain £250 of the deposit to cover cleaning and repair costs. The balance of the deposit (£750) is returned to the tenant in October 2011.

Bill spends £180 having the carpets professionally cleaned and £75 having the door repaired.

Bill prepares accounts for the property rental business to 31 March each year.

When preparing accounts for the year to 31 March 2012, Bill must include as income the £250 retained from the tenant. However, he can deduct the actual cost of cleaning the property (£180) and repairing the door (£75). As the amount actually spent (£255) exceeds the amount retained, he is given relief for the additional £5 in computing the profits of his property rental business.

The balance of the deposit returned to the tenant is not taken into account as income of the business.

As stated in the article on use of the property rental toolkit in our September issue, HMRC recognise that accounting for deposits can sometimes cause problems. Guidance on income that should be taken into account in computing the profits of a property rental business can be found in their Property Income Manual at PIM1052 (see https://www.gov.uk/hmrc-internal-manuals/property-income-manual/pim1052).

17.3.   Holding Deposit

Holding deposits are another form of deposit commonly taken by landlords, particularly in periods where the letting market is buoyant and demand for property is high. As the name suggests, a holding deposit is paid by the tenant to secure the property while the tenancy agreement is signed. In return, the landlord will take the property off the market.

A holding deposit is usually in the region of one week's rent. The terms governing the use of the deposit and the circumstances in which it may be retained by the landlord should be set out in a holding deposit agreement so all parties know where they stand.

In the event that the let falls through and under the terms of the agreement the landlord retains some or all of the deposit as compensation for the inconvenience and costs incurred in relation to the prospective let, the amount of the retained deposit should be included as income of the property rental business. However, the landlord would be able to claim a deduction for any costs actually incurred in relation to aborted let, such as advertising or legal fees.

In the event that the let goes ahead, the holding deposit would either be returned to the tenant or used to form part of the security deposit (see above). If the holding deposit is returned, it does not form part of the income of the business. Where the holding deposit is used as part of the security deposit, as explained above, it is only taken into account to the extent that it is retained by the landlord to cover damage etc. at the end of the let.

17.3.1. Practical Tip

As a general rule, deposits taken from tenants only form part of the income of the property rental business to the extent that the deposit is ultimately retained by the landlord. Any deposits that are merely held on the tenant's behalf before being returned to the tenant are not taken into account as income. On the other side of the coin, a deduction is given for any costs actually incurred by the landlord in making good damage etc. covered under the terms of the deposit agreement.

17.4.   Tax Treatment Of 'Gifted Deposits'?

A recent case before the First-tier Tribunal (Day and Anor v Revenue & Customs [2015] UKFTT 142 (TC)) holds some valuable lessons for landlords selling a buy-to-let property.

One of the properties in the above case had been sold using a 'gifted deposit' scheme.

17.4.1. Gifted Deposit Schemes

These schemes used to be very popular and were promoted as a way of becoming a property owner without having to come up with any of the purchase price. The seller of the property would agree to take (say) 5% less than the asking price (which was itself often a somewhat inflated one), but this would be done by the seller making a 'gift' to the buyer of the 5% difference. The buyer could then obtain a 95% mortgage on the stated purchase price, but the other 5% was provided by the seller so the buyer had none of their own money invested in the property.

Everyone seemed quite relaxed about this practice, even though to me it looked very much like a fraud on the lender of the money if they were not informed about the 'gift'. I recall raising this with a senior manager at one of the high street banks and asking what he thought about it. He asked me one question: 'In this hypothetical situation, does the buyer keep up with the mortgage payments?' When I replied 'yes', he gave me his professional opinion: 'Why should I care, then?'

This particular scheme was operated in the above case with the full knowledge of the lender involved – indeed the scheme was organised by the Halifax. Under the scheme, Mr Day and his co-investor effectively paid the 5% deposit on the sale to themselves, purportedly on behalf of the buyers, and the Halifax provided the buyers with a loan of the other 95% of the sale price. The point was to enable the Halifax to lend the buyers the whole of the actual purchase price whilst being able to record it as a 95% mortgage rather than a 100% one.

17.4.2. Tax Treatment

HMRC contended that the sale proceeds for capital gains tax (CGT) purposes should be the whole amount shown in the sale documentation (£66,300), rather than the price after the 'gifted deposit' of £62,985.

The Tribunal described the £66,300 as 'a label' and agreed that the correct sale proceeds were the amount after the gifted deposit - £62,985.

The important point, however, was what they said about gifted deposits in general and their view of the rights and wrongs of them. In the Day case, the gifted deposit had been paid with the full knowledge (indeed, with the encouragement) of the Halifax, the lender concerned. The Tribunal suggested their view might have been very different if the deposit had been 'gifted' without the lender's knowledge (as many were when this was a popular ruse in the buy-to-let market).

They did not mince their words, either:

"If the appellants had fraudulently paid the deposit in order to help the purchasers obtain a 95% mortgage, we might well not have been persuaded that the appellants could rely on that fraud to reduce their tax liability."

The thing that saved Mr Day and his co-investor was that this was one of the 'respectable' gifted deposits, because the lender concerned knew about it and indeed was promoting it. Things might have been very different if it had been one of the 'under the counter' schemes that were around at the time.

17.4.3. Practical Tip

If you bought a property using a gifted deposit scheme, the correct purchase price for CGT purposes when you come to sell it is likely to be the price net of the gifted deposit.

If anyone suggests using a gifted deposit, make certain the lender is fully aware of what is going on, and agrees to it.

18. Cash Basis v Accruals Basis

Under Generally Accepted Accounting Practice (GAAP) – the accounting rules and standards that govern financial reporting -- profits must be worked out using the accruals basis. The accruals basis, which is sometimes referred to as the `earnings basis', recognises income earned in a period and expenditure incurred in a period.

It does not matter whether the amounts have been received or paid in the period. The income and expenditure is matched to the period to which each relate, rather than to the time at which the income was received or when the payments were made.

This means that under the accruals basis it is necessary to take account of money owed (debtors) and money (owing) and also prepayments and accruals.

By contrast, the cash basis works essentially on the basis of cash in and cash out. Income is recognised when payment is received and expenditure is recognised when payment is made. The cash basis is a simpler basis and requires less adjustments at the year-end.

For example, there is no need to calculate prepayments and accruals as there is under the accruals basis.

Further, tax is only assessed on profits that have been realised.

The timing difference between the accruals basis and cash basis is illustrated by the following simple example.

Cash Basis v Accrual Basis

A business prepares accounts to 31 March each year.

On 13 March 2018 the business issues an invoice for £1,000, and on 28 March 2018 it issues an invoice for £4,000. Both relate to work done in March 2018. The invoice dated 13 March is paid on 29 March 2018 and the invoice dated 28 March 2018 is paid on 2 May 2018.

The company also receives a bill for £750 on 2 March 2018, which it pays on 23 March 2018, and a bill for £500, which it pays on 14 April 2018.

Under the accrual basis, both invoices will be taken into account in computing the profit for the 2017/18 and relief will be given for the expenses of £750 and £500.

By contrast, under the cash basis, only the invoice for £1,000 for which payment was received on 29 March 2018 and the bill of £750 paid on 23 March 2018 will be taken into account in working out the profit for 2017/18.

Payment of the invoice dated 28 March 2018 was not received until 2nd May 2018 and will, therefore, be taken into account in calculating the profit for 2018/19. Likewise, the bill for £500 paid on 14 April 2018 will be deducted in computing the profits for 2018/19, as the cash was paid out in that year.

18.1.   Cash Basis For Traders

Since 6 April 2013, traders meeting the eligibility conditions have been able to choose to use the cash basis to work out their business profits. Prior to 6 April 2017, the cash basis was open to traders with turnover below the VAT registration threshold for the year.

However, as part of the reforms designed to ease the transition to a digital tax age, the cash basis entry threshold was increased to £150,000 from 6 April 2017, thereby extending availability of the cash basis to many more traders from 2017/18. The threshold is doubled for Universal Credit Claimants.

Use of the cash basis is voluntary and eligible traders wishing to use the cash basis must elect to do so. Once a trader makes a cash basis election, he or she must use the cash basis for all trades that they carry on in that tax year.

An election has effect for the year in which it is made and subsequent years. In practice, the trader who wishes to remain in the cash basis simply ticks the relevant box on his or her self-assessment return.

If a trader wants to leave the cash scheme, for example, if circumstances change and the accruals basis is more beneficial (for example, if they wish to claim sideways loss relief), they can elect to do so.

This can be achieved by not ticking the cash basis box on the self-assessment tax return. As the cash basis is designed as a simplification measure for smaller businesses, a business must leave the cash basis in the tax year following that in which receipts from all trades exceed the exit threshold.

The exit threshold is set at twice the entry threshold – so at £300,000 from 2017/18 (and at twice the VAT registration threshold for earlier tax years). See section 24 for adjustments that may be required when a trader leaves the cash basis.

The cash basis is available to unincorporated businesses only – companies must use the accruals basis to work out profits. Certain other businesses are excluded from using the cash basis, including partnerships which have one or more corporate partners.

18.2.   Legislation And Guidance

The legislation governing the use of the cash basis for traders is found in ITTOIA 2005, Pt. 2, Ch. 3A. HMRC guidance can be found on Self-Assessment Helpsheet HS222 (see www.gov.uk/government/publications/how-to-calculate-your-taxable-profits-hs222-self-assessment-helpsheet). More detailed guidance can be found in HMRC's Business Income Manual at BIM 70000ff (see www.gov.uk/hmrc-internal-manuals/business-income-manual/bim70000).

18.3. Extension Of Cash Basis To Unincorporated Property Businesses

From 6 April 2017, the availability of the cash basis is extended to unincorporated property businesses whose rental income does not exceed the eligibility threshold, which is set at £150,000.

Property companies cannot use the cash basis and must continue to prepare accounts on the accruals basis. Unlike traders, for unincorporated property business the cash basis is the default basis where the eligibility conditions are met, and consequently landlords eligible to use the cash basis must elect for the accruals basis if they do not want to use the cash basis to prepare their accounts. By contrast, eligible traders wishing to use the cash basis must elect to do so.

Most landlords are individuals and as long as the eligibility criteria are met, the cash basis will apply unless they opt for the accruals basis. Likewise, partnerships can use the cash basis (as long as rental income is not above the threshold) if the partnership comprises only of individuals; those with one or more corporate partners are excluded from the cash basis, as are limited liability partnerships.

The availability of the cash basis is not limited to UK property businesses – it is also available in respect of overseas property businesses and furnished holiday lettings where the eligibility criteria (see Section 6) are met. Eligible non-residents landlords would also be within the scope of the cash basis.

Legislation extending the cash basis to landlords was introduced by F(No. 2)A 2017, s. 16 and Schedule 2 and, in the main, the provisions are found in ITTOIA 2005, s. 271A to 271E.

The cash basis for landlord's legislation relies on some but not all of the provisions that govern the use of the cash basis by traders (as contained in ITTOIA 2005, Pt. 2, Ch. 3A). However, the cash basis for landlords' legislation contains some additional provisions relevant only to landlords.

18.4. Cash Basis By Default

Not only was the cash basis extended to unincorporated property businesses from 6 April 2017, it also became the default basis. Consequently, an eligible property business meeting the cash basis eligibility tests set out in Section 6 below will be required to use the cash basis unless they opt out of doing so.

Consequently, it is the cash basis rather than the accruals basis that is the norm for smaller property businesses. However, that is not to say that landlords don't have a choice as to whether they prepare their accounts using the cash basis – they do. It is just that in the absence of any action to the contrary, the cash basis will apply to eligible landlords by default. The option remains for a landlord to continue to use the accruals basis – however, he or she must opt to do so.

Larger unincorporated property businesses whose receipts are in excess of the £150,000 cash basis ceiling will not have a choice. Their default will remain the accruals basis; they will not need to opt out of the cash basis as it will not be available to them. Also, any landlord failing to meet any of the other eligibility tests, even if their rental receipts are below the £150,000 ceiling, must also continue to prepare accounts using the accruals basis.

The first step is to ascertain whether the cash basis applies by default by applying each of the tests set out in Section 5 below. If having applied the tests, the cash basis applies, it is necessary to determine whether this is the preferred basis and, if not, to opt out so that profits can be prepared using the accruals basis.

18.5.   Eligibility – The Cash Basis Tests

The legislation for determining whether the cash basis applies to a landlord by default is framed in the form of five tests – A, B, C, D and E. If *none* of the tests is met, the cash basis applies by default. However, if *any* of the tests is met, the business will not be eligible to use the cash basis and must continue to prepare accounts by reference to the accruals basis.

A

Test A is met if the business is carried on at any time in the tax year by:

- a company;

- a limited liability partnership;

- a corporate firm;

- the trustees of a trust; or

- the personal representatives of a person.

A partnership is treated as a `corporate firm' (and thus not eligible for the cash basis) if a partner in the firm is not an individual.

B

Test B is met if the cash basis receipts for the year exceed £150,000.

The cash basis receipts are those that are taken into account in working out the profits of the property business on a cash basis. This is explored further in Section 13 below.

This test limits the availability of the cash basis to smaller property businesses with receipts of £150,000 a year or less. Larger property businesses with receipts in excess of this limit are excluded from the cash basis and must continue to use the accruals basis to work out profits.

C

Where individuals who are married or in a civil partnership and who live together own property jointly, for income tax purposes, the income is split equally between them (by virtue of ITA 2007, s. 836).

Condition C prevents the cash basis from applying where a landlord receives a share of joint property income (treated as arising to the joint owners in equal shares under ITA 2007, s. 836) and the profits of another person (i.e. the landlord's spouse or civil partner) also receiving a share of that joint property income are calculated in accordance with Generally Accepted Accounting Principles (GAAP). Where this is the case, the individual must also use the accruals basis to calculate profits in accordance with GAAP.

This test means that where a property is owned jointly by spouses or civil partners, they must use the same basis to compute their profits. Consequently, if one party is not eligible for the cash basis, the cash basis is not available to the other party in respect of the property business receiving a share of the joint income.

D

A landlord is also prohibited from using the cash basis if condition D applies. This test is met if a Business Premises Renovation Allowance is made in calculating the profits of the business property business and a balancing event in the year would give rise to a balancing adjustment. Where this is the case, profits must be computed using the accruals basis in accordance with GAAP.

E

Test E is only relevant where none of A, B, C or D are met.

Test E is that the landlord has opted out of the cash basis by electing for the accruals basis to apply.

Unless such an election is made and none of tests A to D is met, the cash basis will apply. However, where an election to opt out of the cash basis is made, the cash basis does not apply and the accruals basis will apply instead.

None of A, B, C, D or E apply

If none of the tests A, B, C or D are met and the landlord has not opted out of the cash basis, the cash basis applies by default.

Flowchart

The position is summarised by the following flowchart.

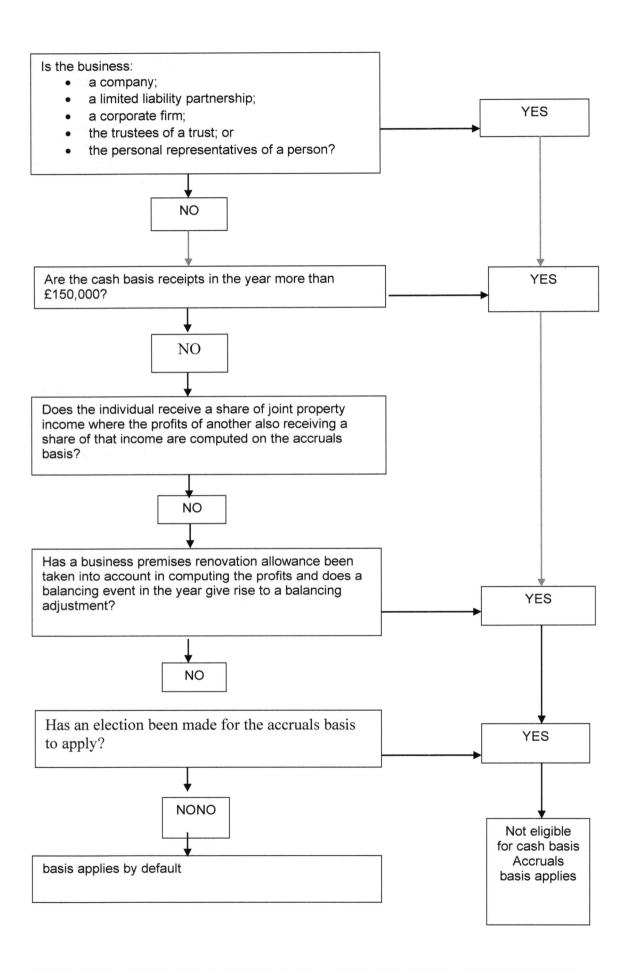

18.6.   Opting For The Accruals Basis

While there are a number of advantages in the cash basis, not every landlord who is eligible for the cash basis will prefer to prepare accounts on this basis. Where tests A to D in section 6 above are met, in the absence of an election, the cash basis will apply by default.

Consequently, if the landlord wishes instead to prepare accounts on the accruals basis (for example, because accruals basis accounts are required by the bank to support a mortgage application), he or she must elect for the cash basis not to apply. This must be done within one year of the normal self-assessment filing date for the tax year.

Opting For Cash Basis Not To Apply

Kevin is a landlord who meets the conditions for the cash basis to apply for 2017/18. The cash basis will apply by default unless Kevin elects otherwise.

However, Kevin has a number of other businesses for which accounts are prepared on the accruals basis and wishes to continue using this basis of preparation for his property business as he is familiar with it and has been using it for many years.

He must elect for the cash basis not to apply. The normal self-assessment filing date for the 2017/18 return is 31 January 2019. Kevin must make the election for the cash basis not to apply by 31 January 2020.

For commentary on the adjustments that may be required where a landlord joins or leaves the cash basis, see, respectively, Section 23 and Section 24.

18.7.   Multiple Property Businesses

Where a landlord has more than one property business, the cash basis test will be applied separately to each business. Where the cash basis applies by default to more than one of those businesses, the landlord will be able to decide in relation to each of those businesses whether to remain in the cash basis or whether to opt out.

This may mean that a landlord prepares accounts on a different basis for different property businesses. This is a departure from the cash basis rules as they apply to traders, as under those rules, where a trader opts for the cash basis for one business, he must also prepare the accounts of other eligible businesses on the cash basis.

The option to mix and match, which is open to property businesses, is not available to traders opting for the cash basis.

The opportunity to make the decision as to whether the cash basis or the accruals basis is more appropriate on business by business basis allows landlords with, say, a UK property business and an overseas property business to stay within the cash basis for one and opt out for the other.

18.8. Joint Owners

In general, individuals who are not married or in a civil partnership and who own property jointly without being in a formal partnership will each be able to decide whether to remain in the cash basis where the cash basis applies by default, or whether to opt for the accruals basis. The decision by one individual is not binding on other individuals and there is no requirement that all joint owners use the same basis.

Joint Owners

Lucy and Karen are cousins. Following the death of their grandmother, they inherit some money which they invest in a 'buy-to-let' property. The property is owned as tenants in common with each having a 50% share.

In 2017/18, the rental income is £800 per month (£9,600 a year), of which each individual receives £4,800. The cash basis applies by default. Each individual is taxed by reference to their share of the profits.

Lucy is happy to work out her taxable profit by reference to the cash basis and remains within the cash basis.

Karen has her own catering business in respect of which she prepares accounts on the accruals basis. She is comfortable with that and decides to work out her property income on that basis and opts out of the cash basis.

Karen and Lucy will be taxed on the profits computed in accordance with the basis they have chosen. This means that despite having equal shares in the property, they will not necessarily have the same taxable profit each year.

This rule is modified in certain circumstances where the joint owners are married or in a civil partnership: see Section 9 below.

It should be noted that the cash basis eligibility threshold (Test B: see Section 6) applies in relation to each individual's share of the rental income, rather than by reference to the total rental income in respect of the jointly-owned properties.

Cash Basis Eligibility

Jake and Josh are brothers. They jointly own a number of properties which they let out. Jake has a 10% share and Josh a 90% share of each property and they split the rent accordingly. In 2017/18, the total rental profits are £200,000, of which £20,000 is allocated to Jake and £180,000 to Josh.

The cash basis eligibility tests are applied to them individually by reference to their share of the profits. Josh meets test B as his profits are more than £150,000, so he is not eligible to use the cash basis and must calculate his taxable profits on an accruals basis.

By contrast, Jake does not meet any of the tests, so the cash basis applies by default and he must calculate his taxable profits on that basis (unless he elects to opt for the accruals basis).

18.9. Joint Owners – Married Couples And Civil Partners

The flexibility of joint owners to each choose whether they apply the cash basis where eligible to do so is restricted in certain cases where the joint owners are married to each other or in a civil partnership.

Test C (see Section 6 above) prevents the cash basis from applying where a person who is carrying on a property business receives a share of joint property income in respect of property owned jointly with that person's spouse or civil partner, and the spouse or civil partner's profits in relation to their share of the income is calculated on the accruals basis in accordance with GAAP.

This rule is to facilitate the existing legislation which treats income from assets jointly-owned by spouses or civil partners as being split 50:50, unless the actual beneficial ownership is not 50:50 and an election has been made to allocate income in accordance with underlying beneficial ownership.

Married Joint Owners

Lois and Luke are married and own several properties jointly. Luke's share of the joint income is computed on accruals basis. Consequently, Lois is not eligible for the cash basis and her profits must also be computed on the accruals basis.

18.10. Calculation Of Property Business Profits On The Cash Basis

As noted above, the cash basis applies by default if none of the conditions set out in section 6 above have been met for the tax year in question (and that tax year is 2017/18 or a later tax year).

Where the cash basis applies, the profits of the property business must be computed in accordance with the cash basis rules, as set out in the legislation.

Under the cash basis, receipts of the business are brought into account at the time that they are received and expenses of the business are brought into account at the time they are paid. This is subject to the adjustments which are authorised or required by law.

18.11. Income

The cash basis does not change the scope of what is treated as property income and where the cash basis applies, receipts treated as property income by virtue of ITTOIA 2005, Pt. 3 under the accruals basis would continue to be treated as receipts of the property income business under the cash basis.

As previously noted, the main difference is one of timing. Income is not counted under the cash basis until it has actually been received. It is the date of receipt that determines the period into which the income falls, rather the period for which it is for. Thus, rent for March 2018 which is received on 14 April 2018 is, under the cash basis, income of 2018/19 as it was received in 2018/19, rather than income of 2017/18, regardless of the fact that the month to which the rent relates (March 2018) falls in that tax year. The income is not matched to the period for which it was earned as under the accruals basis – all that is relevant is the date on which it was received.

However, it should be noted that where a letting agent is used, the date of receipt for cash basis purposes is the date that the rental income is received by the letting agent, rather than the date on which the letting agent pays the money over to the landlord. The letting agent acts on behalf of the landlord and collects the rent on the landlord's behalf.

Where the cash basis applies, amounts that are treated as falling within the capital gains tax regime, such as premiums on long leases and the proceeds from the sale of the property itself, continue to be assessed to tax by virtue of the capital gains tax rules rather than being brought into account at the time of receipt as income under the cash basis.

However, because of the different rules for treating capital items under the cash basis (which are explained in Section 17 below, there will be some receipts that are brought into account under the cash basis, but which do not count as property receipts under the accruals basis. An example for this would be the proceeds received from the sale of a van used in the property business where the cost of that van was deducted as an expense under the cash basis when the van was originally acquired.

18.12. Expenditure

Under the cash basis, expenses are recognised when paid – they are not matched to the period to which they relate as under the accruals basis. Consequently, there is no need to worry about prepayments and accruals. However, there is no difference in the type of revenue expenses that are deductible – only in the time when relief is given (although different rules apply to capital expenditure).

As under the accruals basis, only expenses which are incurred wholly and exclusively for the purposes of the property income business can be deducted under the cash basis.

Common expenses that are deductible in computing profits include letting agent's fees, advertising costs, cleaning costs, landlord's insurance, stationery, postage and printing costs, staff costs and such like.

For the treatment and deductibility of capital expenditure under the cash basis, see Section 18.16.

Deduction Of Expenses

James has a flat which he lets out. In 2017/18, he is eligible for the cash basis. In March 2018, he receives a bill for cleaning of £80 on 2 March which he pays on 21 March, a bill from the letting agent of £200 on 18 March in respect of managing the property for the period from 15 February 2018 to 14 March 2018, which he pays on 6 April, and a bill from his gardener for tidying the garden for £50 on 28 March, which he settles that day.

Under the cash basis, James would be able to deduct expenses in respect of cleaning (paid on 21 March) and gardening (paid on 28 March) in computing the 2017/18 profits. By contrast, the bill for the management fees would be deductible in computing the profits for the 2018/19 as the bill was not paid until the 2018/19 tax year. Under the cash basis the period to which the bill relates is not relevant – only the date on which the cash was paid out.

Where a letting agent is used and the letting agents meets expenses on the landlord's behalf, under the cash basis the expenditure is treated as incurred on the date that the letting agent pays the expense rather than that on which it is recovered from the landlord or deducted from the rent received from the tenant before paying the balance over to the landlord. The letting agent acts on behalf of the landlord.

18.13. No Accruals And Prepayments Or Debtors Or Creditor

As the cash basis works only on cash in and cash out without matching income and expenses to the period in question, there is no need to take account of money owed by debtors or to creditors or to calculate accruals and pre-payments. As a result, the cash basis is far more straightforward and simplifies the job of calculating taxable profits.

18.14. Lease Premiums

Where a landlord calculates profits under the cash basis, receipts of lease premiums and other sums treated as premiums are simply recognised as income when they are received. However, following the cash basis rules for trading income, payment of premiums or other sums treated as premiums are not deductible as an expense.

18.15. Security Deposits

When a landlord lets a property, the landlord will generally take a security deposit from the tenant as a contingency against damage to the property or furniture, etc. The deposit is returned to the tenant at the end of the lease, less any amounts that the landlord is eligible to keep under the terms of the lease, for example, to cover repairs. Where the let is a residential let, the deposit is normally protected in a Government-backed tenancy deposit scheme.

In some cases, the landlord passes the deposit over to the scheme for the duration of the tenancy; in other cases, the landlord retains the deposit and pays a fee to the scheme.

Applying the cash basis strictly would necessitate recognising the deposit as income when it is received and allowing relief as expenditure when it is returned to the tenant. However, this would result in the landlord being taxed on the deposit at the start of the tenancy and not receiving relief for the return of the deposit to the tenant until the end of the tenancy, which may be some years later.

Consequently, landlords are only required to account for any part of the security deposit which is retained, for example to meet the cost of repairs, once it has been established that it is legally the landlord's property.

18.16. Capital Expenditure

Under the accruals basis, no deduction is allowed for capital expenditure. Instead, relief for some capital expenditure is given in the form of capital allowances. Otherwise, capital expenditure is taken into account in computing any eventual capital gain or loss on disposal.

Simpler rules for dealing with capital expenditure were introduced alongside the cash basis. From 6 April 2017, most items of capital expenditure can be deducted (on a date paid basis) in computing the cash basis profits of the property income business. This gives immediate relief for the expenditure against profits. However, certain types of capital expenditure do not qualify for deduction.

No deduction is allowed for capital expenditure that is incurred on or in connection with the acquisition or disposal of a business or part of a business.

Likewise, no deduction is available in respect of expenditure on an item of a capital nature which is incurred on or in connection with the provision, alteration or disposal of:
- any asset that is not a depreciating asset;
- any asset that is not acquired for use on a continuing basis in the trade;
- a car;
- land;

- a non-qualifying intangible asset, including education or training; or
- a financial asset.

A depreciating asset is one which within 20 years is either no longer of use as a business asset or has a value of ten per cent or less of its value at the time that the expenditure on it was originally incurred.

The rules mean that, unsurprisingly, a landlord would not be allowed to deduct the cost of purchasing a property which is let out – as usual, gains or losses are dealt with under the capital gains tax rules. However, where he buys a capital item, such as say office furniture, the cost of that furniture can be deducted by reference to the date of payment when computing the cash basis profits of the property income business.

Where the let is a residential let, relief for expenditure on replacement domestic items is given in accordance with the rules explained in Section 18.17 below.

If a deduction has been given for the cost of the capital item, in the event that the item is subsequently sold, the sale proceeds are taken into account as a receipt of the property income business when the cash is received.

Treatment Of Capital Expenditure

Bobby is a landlord who from 2017/18 computes the profits of his property income business using the cash basis.

In August 2017, he buys a van for use in the business. The van costs £15,000. The cost of the van is deducted in computing the profits for 2017/18.

In May 2020, he sells the van for £5,000. The proceeds are treated as a receipt of the property business in computing the profits for 2020/21.

18.17. Replacement Of Domestic Items

Where the let is a residential let, other than a furnished holiday letting, the normal relief for the replacement of domestic items applies where profits are computed on the cash basis. Under these rules a deduction is given for expenditure on replacement items of furniture, furnishing, appliances (including white goods) used in the let property.

The amount which is eligible for deduction is relation to the replacement item is the cost of the replacement item, plus any associated costs of acquiring the new item (such as delivery) or disposing of the old item, less any proceeds received in respect of the disposal of the old item. The cost is capped at the cost of an equivalent standard replacement to the original – where the replacement is superior, the `improvement' element is not deductible.

Unlike other types of lettings, capital allowances can be claimed in respect of fixtures and fittings in a furnished holiday let. Consequently, the relief for replacement of domestic items described above is not in point.

18.18. Capital Allowances – Cars

Under the cash basis, capital allowances are not generally available. Relief for capital expenditure is instead given by deduction (see Section 18.16 for details). However, cars are the exception to this rule and capital allowances are available for cars used in the property business computed in the usual way.

It should be noted that where a deduction for vehicle costs is computed by reference to a mileage rate (see Section 18.19), capital allowances cannot be claimed for cars.

18.19. Mileage Rates

Landlords (regardless of whether they use the cash basis or not) can opt to use fixed rate per business mile to calculate their allowable deductions for motoring expenses rather than deducting actual running costs and claiming capital allowances. The option for landlords to use mileage rates was announced at the time of the 2017 Autumn Budget and is available from 6 April 2017 onwards. However, corporate landlords or those in a partnership with individual and non-individual members are not able to claim mileage rates.

The mileage rates are the same as those available to traders – 45p per mile for the first 10,000 business miles and 25p per mile for any subsequent business miles in the tax year for cars and vans and 24p per mile for motorcycles. Where a landlord has claimed capital allowances in respect of a car or a deduction for the cost of a van or motorcycle under the capital expenditure rules, mileage allowances cannot be claimed for that vehicle. This is because the mileage rates allow for depreciation.

Transitional arrangements are available to landlords who claimed capital allowances in relation to a vehicle in the period 2013/14 to 2016/17 and who wish to start claiming mileage allowances for the same vehicles for 2017/18. The transitional arrangements prevent any further deductions for capital allowances once mileage allowances are claimed.

18.20. Relief For Interest

Relief for interest and financing costs incurred in relation to the property business is given in the same way under the cash basis as under the accruals basis.

Where the property is a residential property, the method of relief is moving from relief by deduction to relief as a basic rate tax deduction. These rules apply equally under the cash basis.

During the transitional period, relief is available as follows:

- for 2017/18, relief for 75% of the interest and finance costs is given by deduction, with relief for the remaining 25% as a basic rate tax reduction;
- for 2018/19 relief for 50% of the interest and finance costs is given by deduction with relief for the remaining 50% as a basic rate tax reduction;
- for 2019/20 relief for 25% of the interest and finance costs is given by deduction with relief for the remaining 75% as a basic rate tax reduction;
- from 2020/21 onwards, relief is given wholly as a basic rate tax reduction.

For non-residential properties and furnished holiday lettings, relief continues to be given by deduction, although landlords are not prevented from using the cash basis where interest costs are more than £500 a year (as is the case under the cash basis rules as they apply to traders).

Relief for interest on loans is capped on loans to the value of the property when first let, if the loan is used for non property business purposes.

18.21. VAT

The cash basis entry threshold (set at £150,000 for 2017/18) is above the VAT registration threshold. Where a property income business is registered for VAT and using the cash basis to calculate profits, income and expenses can be recorded either including or excluding VAT – but whichever method is used, it must be used for both income and expenses.

Where income and expenses are recorded including VAT, payments of VAT made to HMRC are treated as an expense and VAT repayments from HMRC are treated as a receipt.

18.22. Entering The Cash Basis

Transitional arrangements apply where a landlord moves from the accruals basis to the cash basis. Because the timing for recognising income and expenditure is different under the cash basis and the accruals basis, the transitional rules are needed to ensure that all income and expenditure is taken into account and also that items are only taken into account once.

When a landlord moves to the cash basis, he or she must take into account all income actually received in the tax year. In the first year of the cash basis where this follows a year on which profits were computed on the accruals it is also necessary to make adjustments:

- where money was owed to the business at the end of the previous year (debtors) and taken into account in computing profits for that year, the money is not taken into account as a receipt when received in a cash basis year; and
- where money was owed to suppliers at the end of the previous year (creditors) and relief was given in computing profits for that year, no deduction is given in the first cash basis year when the bill is paid.

As capital allowances are only available in respect of cars under the cash basis, an adjustment is also needed where items (other than cars) are not fully written off. The written down value is treated as an expense in the first year of the cash basis.

18.23. Leaving The Cash Basis

In the event that a landlord has been preparing accounts on a cash basis moves back to the accruals basis, adjustments will be needed when the landlord leaves the cash basis to ensure no items are omitted or counted twice. A landlord may leave the cash basis either because he opts to do so or because he is no longer eligible for the cash basis, for example, if the business has expanded and rental receipts exceed the exit threshold (set at £300,000 from 2017/18).

18.24. Planning And Timing Issues

Under the cash basis, income is only recognised when it is received and expenditure when paid. From a tax perspective, this means that the landlord will not have to pay tax on income before it has been received and also that relief is automatically given for bad debts. On the other side of the coin, relief for expenditure is not given until the payment has been made. This may mean that relief is given in a later tax year under the cash basis than under the accruals basis.

Relief for expenditure can be accelerated by making the payment early or advancing the expenditure to bring it into an earlier tax year – for example, paying a bill on 28 March 2018 rather than on 10 April 2018 will mean relief is given in 2017/18 rather than in 2018/19.

Where the cash basis applies, the desire to delay tax on income and advance relief on expenditure creates something of a conflict with good cashflow management. The tax rules benefit income being received as late as possible and payments being made as early as possible, whereas from a cashflow perspective the opposite is true. As always, the tax tail should not be allowed to wag the dog.

18.25. Final Thoughts

The extension of the cash basis to landlords is introduced as a simplification measure with a view to easing the transition to digital recording and reporting. This will be welcomed by many landlords as is more straightforward than the accruals basis.

The cash basis is not for all landlords. Where a landlord is eligible, he or she will need to assess whether it is for them, and opt out if it is not.

It is important to remember that the cash basis is the default basis for eligible landlords and that if you do nothing and meet the eligibility tests, this is the basis that you must use. Under the new rules, the cash basis is king.

Companies And Property Taxes

19. Can A Limited Company Improve YOUR Tax Position?

In this section you will learn whether holding your properties through a company will benefit your tax position.

19.1.   The Most Commonly Asked Tax Questions

'Should I buy my property through a limited company?'

'Should I move my properties into a limited company?'

'Is it true that I can save tax by holding my properties in a limited company?'

I am sure that, like most investors, you will have either asked or been involved in a discussion where these questions have been debated.

In all fairness, the answer to these kinds of questions depends on the following three key factors:

a) your chosen investment strategy;
b) your personal and financial circumstances/ambitions;
c) how long you intend to hold on to the properties.

However, before you even decide whether a limited company will improve your tax position, there are some very basic rules and guidelines that must be understood.

19.2.   Transferring Properties Into A Limited Company

Do you already own investment properties?

Are you already on the buy-to-let investment ladder?

If the answer is yes, and you are now considering whether moving your properties into a limited company will save you tax, then consider the following FACT:

Properties must be transferred into a Limited Company at market value, unless a portfolio exists that is deemed to constitute a 'business'.

Yes, that's right!

Generally speaking, moving properties into a company is treated in the same way as if you were selling the properties.

If you bought your investment property ten years ago and you would now like to move it into a limited company, then you are likely to have to pay an *immediate* capital gains tax liability.

This is due to the fact that property prices have significantly increased over the past few years.

The exception to this rule is if the property is your **principle private residence**.

Transferring Properties into a Limited Company

Alex bought five investment properties, and their combined purchase value was £250,000.

Some years later they are worth a combined total of £550,000; that is, the combined value of his portfolio has more than doubled!

This means that his capital gain is £300,000.

By transferring the properties into a company, he may be liable to pay tax at both 18% and 28% on this amount, which means that he will have an immediate and significant tax liability (excluding any reliefs).

19.3.   Don't Forget Stamp Duty!

Another 'tax bombshell' that may well hit when transferring properties into a ltd company could be stamp duty. Stamp duty land tax (SDLT) is charged on the market value of the properties being transferred into the company, even if gifted for no consideration, if the company is connected to the individual transferring the properties, which it usually is. If a number of properties are being transferred together, there is a new rule which says that the amount of SDLT charged is averaged out, as long as it is not less than 1%. Nevertheless, SDLT will be payable.

> **Do not** start to form a limited company before you know what your tax liability will be.

19.4.   Understanding 'Limited Liability'

There is a common misunderstanding by many property investors who believe that if they hold their properties in a limited company, they will escape from the banks/creditors if anything goes wrong.

As a separate legal entity, the company is, in theory, responsible for its own debts and liabilities. However, it is *very likely* that any lender will insist on a personal guarantee from the directors or shareholders when lending to the company. This means that if the company fails, the directors *will be liable*!

Consider the following case study.

When Limited Liability Will Not Help You

Mr and Mrs Prone form the limited company ABC Ltd. They borrow 75% of the purchase price and proceed to rent out the property through the company. They withdraw every penny of rent received without considering any tax consequences.

At the end of the first year the mortgage company decides to repossess the property as the mortgage has not been paid for six months.

In the above case study, the directors will be held responsible for paying

- the outstanding mortgage;
- corporation tax on the profits;
- any tax due on the money that they have withdrawn.

This is because the liabilities have arisen as a direct result of their actions.

By law, directors are largely responsible for the actions of the company, and hence if it all goes wrong, there is a fair chance that the directors will find themselves personally liable for any debts arising as a result of their decisions.

However, having the cover of **limited liability** can still be useful if the business incurs unexpected (i.e., outside the control of the directors) losses or liabilities.

Such losses and liabilities can occur when

- a property development goes horribly wrong;
- tenants refuse to move out, and the company runs out of cash to pay the mortgage;
- interest rates suddenly double;
- the housing market crashes (let's hope this doesn't happen!);
- a tenant is injured on your property and successfully sues the company for personal injury.

This last pointer is a very good reason for ensuring that you have the correct landlord's insurance in place.

Let's look at another case study to illustrate the point.

Using Limited Liability to Your Advantage

Mr and Mrs Prone decide to enter the buy-to-let market and set up a limited company to hold the property. The property costs £100,000, and a loan is obtained from the bank for 85% of the purchase price.

Tenants are found and a rental agreement signed. No insurance is taken out as it is not considered a priority.

Three months later, a solicitor's letter arrives claiming that the tenant has fallen down the stairs as a result of improper maintenance of the stairways (there is a hole in one of the stairs).

After much debate and a court case, compensation is set at £150,000. The directors are cleared of any responsibility in the case by the judge. Clearly, the company cannot pay this amount of money, and the company is put into liquidation.

In the above case study, the owners have been successful in that the limited liability of the company has saved them from being personally responsible for the costs.

If this had not been in place, then the costs would have fallen on them, which would have resulted in them having to sell their own houses to meet the claim.

19.5. Two Major Tax Benefits Of Using A Limited Company

As a general rule, if you intend to re-invest the money you have made through your property investments, e.g., you want to continue re-investing the profits into acquiring more properties, then it will be beneficial to invest through a limited company.

There are two *significant* tax benefits of growing a property portfolio through a company. These are explained below.

a) Lower-rate tax savings.

As a higher-rate taxpayer, you pay 40% on your profit and gains. For a limited company the corporation tax rate is currently 20%. This is going down to 19% from April 2017 onwards.

b) Stamp duty savings.

You only pay stamp duty at a rate of 0.5% when purchasing company shares[1].

19.6. Other Benefits/Drawbacks Of A Limited Company

19.6.1. Benefits

Here are some more favourable tax benefits to consider when deciding whether to own your properties through a limited company.

---

[1] This only applies when purchasing a company that already owns the property. It does not apply when a company purchases a property.

- A company can define its own accounting period that does not exceed 12 months.

- Indexation relief is still available for any capital gains, but as from Jan 2018 indexation has been frozen at the Dec 2017 level.

- You will see lower tax rates as companies pay tax at 20%, going down to 19% from April 2017.

- Properties can be transferred within group companies without incurring a tax liability[2].

- You can grow a portfolio more quickly within a company by continuing to re-invest

- Dividends can be extracted from a company in a tax efficient way.

- The rules that restrict interest relief for residential landlords do not apply to companies.

19.6.2. Drawbacks

Here are some drawbacks that you should consider before deciding to own your properties through a limited company.

- Companies cannot use the annual personal CGT allowance. £12,000 for 2019-2020.

- Official company accounts must be produced. The cost of drawing up such accounts can be three to four times more expensive than having your sole trader accounts drawn up.

- Banks are less willing to lend money if you are purchasing through a company.

---

[2]This only applies in a group situation, e.g., a holding company with a 75% subsidiary or subsidiaries.

20. Does Incorporation Stack Up For Landlords?

20.1. Why Should I Incorporate?

At risk of stating the blindingly obvious, <u>a BTL investor should only incorporate his or her business if there is good reason to do so</u>. Before the new rules restricting tax relief for finance costs on residential property, many landlords would not have been better off by incorporating. Since April 2016 a new, more punitive regime for taxing dividend income means that incorporation is even less beneficial.

Example: Sole proprietor vs company

Boris owns several properties, but has no other sources of income. His net property profits are £40,000. In 2016/17, his personal tax position will be:

2016/17	£	£
Rental Income	40,000	40,000
Less: Personal Allowance	(11,000)	
	29,000	
Taxed at:	20%	
Tax		(5,800)
Net income		34,200

If he had instead put his properties into a company, the company would first have to pay corporation tax on its profits:

2016/17	£	£
Rental Income	40,000	40,000
Less: Boris' salary (say)	(8,000)	(8,000)
	32,000	
Taxed at:	20%	
Tax		(6,400)
Net company income		25,600

But this is only half the story; although it is Boris' company, he has so far drawn out only £8,000 salary and the rest of the company's profits are locked up in the company's bank account – those funds are not yet his. He therefore pays a dividend out of the company to put the funds at his personal disposal:

2016/17	£	£
Company funds now payable as dividends:	25,600	25,600
Balance of Boris' Personal Allowance	(3,000)	
Taxable	22,600	
Taxed at:		

		£	£
New Dividend "Allowance" 0%	5,000	-	
Ordinary Dividend Rate 7.5%	17,600	1,320	
	22,600		
Total Income Tax on dividends			(1,320)
Boris' dividend income after tax:			24,280
Add: salary already taken (as above)			8,000
Boris' net income			32,280
Boris' net income if he'd never bothered with a company (above):			34,200
Lost from running portfolio through a company:			(1,920)

Of course the real problem is that, by 2020/21, Boris will be getting only 20% tax relief on his mortgage interest if he continues to hold the property personally, while the corporate alternative would not be caught. Let's suppose that Boris' net rental income of £40,000 is <u>after</u> having paid £32,000 in mortgage interest, and move forwards to 2020/21, where all of his mortgage interest will be subject to the new tax relief restriction:

2020/21		£	£
Rental Income		40,000	40,000
Disallow: interest		32,000	
		72,000	
Less: Personal Allowance		(12,500)	
Deemed taxable:		59,500	
Basic Rate 20%	37,500	7,500	
Higher Rate 40%	22,000	8,800	
	59,500		
Mortgage Interest adjustment		(6,400)	
			(9,900)
Net income			30,100

Boris stands to lose £4,100 by 2020/21 if he continues to run his business personally, even though personal tax-free bands and allowances have risen significantly by then.

We already have a rough idea of how Boris would fare with a corporate property portfolio, because companies will not be affected by the new BTL finance restrictions. On the basis that companies remain static, then Boris would still be £1,920 worse off in a company in 2020/21 than with a personal portfolio now in 2016/17, but that would nevertheless be £2,180 better than sticking with personal ownership all the way through to 2020/21.

Another factor to consider is that the dividend tax free allowance drops from £5,000 per year, in tax year 2017-18, to £2,000 per year, from tax year 2018-19 onwards.

Many career landlords are dealing with much larger numbers, and the savings will be much more substantial. The key consideration is how much the artificial tax cost of disallowing interest, etc., exceeds the compensating 20% tax relief. If we look instead at an alternative where Boris' mortgage interest is only £12,000, the results are quite different:

2020/21		£	£
Rental Income		40,000	40,000
Disallow: interest		12,000	
		52,000	
Less: Personal Allowance		(12,500)	
Deemed taxable:		39,500	
Basic Rate 20%	37,500	7,500	
Higher Rate 40%	2,000	800	
	39,500		
Mortgage Interest adjustment		(2,400)	
			(5,900)
Net income			34,100

In this scenario, the new mortgage interest regime will end up costing Boris only a very small amount annually, even when fully implemented in 2020/21. He would be much better off sticking with direct ownership, rather than incorporating his business.

20.2.   Why Is Incorporation Relief Useful?

Many landlords will have held property for years – decades, even. Such portfolios tend to have increased very significantly in value – they may now be worth (say) two or three times what the landlord originally paid for them. Landlords in this position will, of course, be aware that those properties will be exposed to CGT if and when they are sold. But many landlords do not realise that this CGT will by default apply even if the property is given away.

> **Example 1: 'Gift' Of Properties To Company**
>
> Bill has four properties that he bought twenty years ago for £200,000; they are now worth £550,000. He knows that if he sells the properties on the open market then he will make a gain of £350,000, so long as he achieves the full asking price.
>
> Bill wants to incorporate his BTL business, to avoid the increased income tax charge. He knows that he could sell his properties to his company, so that the company owes him £550,000. He understands that he will have made a capital gain of £350,000, even though he is selling to his own company.
>
> So, Bill decides to give the properties to his company instead. Unfortunately for Bill, tax law basically says HMRC is entitled to its slice of CGT even if Bill doesn't take any money: this is not a bad bargain but a deliberate arrangement by Bill to transfer at undervalue. The transaction is taxable as if Bill had sold at the full market value of £550,000 – Bill will have to pay tax on a capital gain of £350,000, even though he has not received any money (see, for example, HMRC's Capital Gains manual at CG14530 et seq).

20.3.   Incorporation Relief Route

> **Example 2: Incorporation Relief**
>
> Ben also has four properties standing at a capital gain of £350,000. Unlike Bill, he is fully aware that a gift can be 'caught' for CGT, so he opts for the incorporation relief route. He sets up a company and arranges for the company to exchange shares in itself for Ben's portfolio.
>
> In effect, Ben's bricks and mortar property wealth is transmuted into paper – his shares in his new company. The company has offered no money or consideration other than shares in itself. Ben therefore claims incorporation relief (under TCGA 1992, s 162), so that his capital gain is now held over into the company shares – there is no capital gain now, but disposing of a fraction of the shares at some later stage will effectively trigger a corresponding fraction of the postponed capital gain (let us suppose that Ben is happy with this, since he intends to hold on to those shares for the long term).

Many readers will be aware that property businesses are *not* guaranteed to qualify for incorporation relief but should do so where their circumstances are sufficiently similar to those in the case of *Ramsay v HMRC* [2013] UKUT 0226 (TCC) (see HMRC's Capital Gains manual at CG65715, but note that this is HMRC's interpretation of the case); Ben's lettings portfolio qualifies as an active 'business' in the context of incorporation relief, so Ben looks forwards to a CGT-free future, presumably with the odd Daiquiri and/or Gin Sling for good measure. Or does he?

20.4.   Mechanics – Transferring Liabilities

The key issue that has not yet been addressed is business liabilities – mortgages, etc. Many landlords will assume that the business liabilities follow the business, and that is commonly the case. But there are implications. HMRC allows that the business' liabilities do not 'count' as consideration when transferred to the company, so incorporation relief is not restricted.

Example 3: Liabilities Transferred But No Relief Restriction

Benjamin has four properties that he bought in 1997 for £200,000, with a £100,000 mortgage. The properties are now worth £550,000, and the mortgage is now £75,000. He has incurred no enhancement expenditure on the properties, so the only deductible amounts for CGT purposes are the original costs of acquisition and any incidental costs to dispose of the assets, etc. (which we shall treat as negligible, for convenience).

Benjamin transfers his four properties into his new company, in exchange for shares and no other consideration. The company also takes on the borrowings. Assuming his BTL portfolio satisfies the relevant criteria to be considered eligible for incorporation relief, the calculation is:

Benjamin's gain is £550,000 - £200,000 = £350,000

The property portfolio is worth £550,000 - £75,000 = £475,000

The CGT cost of the shares in this simple example is their market value, less the gain now postponed: £475,000 - £350,000 = £125,000 (i.e. Benjamin's own base cost, net of finance)

The gain is held over in full. Benjamin will have a relatively low base cost to his shares as and when he comes to sell or otherwise dispose of them, but he has avoided any CGT now, on incorporation.

However, the amount of the gain that can be held over under incorporation relief *is* restricted where the gain exceeds the net value of the assets transferred.

Example 4: Liabilities Transferred But Relief Restriction Arises

Benito also has four properties that cost him £200,000 and are now worth £550,000. The gain is therefore £350,000, as before (again, ignoring any incidental costs and assuming there was no enhancement expenditure).

However, Benito has bought his properties over a period of several years, starting roughly 15 years ago, and borrowing heavily against his 'earlier' properties to finance the later additions. His borrowings now stand at £250,000 – more than the aggregate original cost of the properties, but still comfortably less than their current value. Benito does, of course, want to transfer his borrowings to the new company – that is the whole point of the incorporation exercise.

Benito's gain is £550,000 - £200,000 = £350,000

The property portfolio is worth £550,000 - £250,000 = £300,000

The CGT cost of the shares on the transfer is their market value less the gain now postponed:

£300,000 - £300,000 (restricted) = £Nil, leaving £50,000 of gain that cannot be postponed through incorporation relief, and that would be assessable on Benito immediately.

20.5.   Paying CGT By Instalments

In this article, we shall look at a potential fall-back option, being the opportunity to pay CGT by instalments, over up to ten years, that *may* help to draw some of the sting of a large CGT bill. There are numerous routes to pay CGT by instalments, but this section will deal only with the issues relevant to transferring BTL property into one's own company.

20.5.1.   Instalment Options – Requirements

If you have no choice but to pay CGT, then it is sometimes possible to pay it over up to ten years by instalments (TCGA 1992, s 281).

The main rules are:
- the assets disposed of must be land (including property) – certain types of shareholding also qualify, but are not really relevant here;
- the disposal must be by way of gift (i.e. transfer for nil consideration, or otherwise than as a bargain at arm's length); and
- that cannot have been 'held over' (i.e. postponed) – e.g. by incorporation relief

Partial relief is permitted – e.g. where incorporation relief is available for some of the gain, then payment by instalments is potentially available for the remainder. This is particularly relevant for those BTL investors contending with latent gains on their BTL portfolio that cannot be postponed (see above).

20.5.2.   Instalment Options – Mechanism

- The taxpayer must make an election to use payments by instalments within four years of the end of the tax year of the gain.
- However, the first instalment is due on the normal date for payment – for individuals, this will currently be 31 January following the tax year of the gain (although the Government is planning that as from April 2020 the payment window for gains on residential property will be 30 days). It would be quite unlikely, therefore, for the taxpayer to wait four years until making the election, if the first instalment is generally due much earlier.
- A further nine instalments fall due on the anniversary of the first.
- Interest is charged on the payment as against the original due date, on each of those instalments.
- A taxpayer may settle the instalment plan early, and have his or her interest re-calculated accordingly.
- If the underlying asset is disposed of for valuable consideration (usually an onward sale for money) by the donee (or indeed any subsequent owner), any outstanding balance of CGT due is payable immediately. This applies where the donor and donee are 'connected persons' (as will be the case for the BTL investor and his own BTL company).

It follows that BTL investors should keep a watchful eye on the disposal by the company of any properties held pre-incorporation, to ensure that they do not inadvertently trigger an immediate charge to any postponed amounts.

Example: Incorporate And Pay CGT By Instalments?

Let's work with the example in the previous article – Benito – who had a 'latent gain' that could not be postponed using incorporation relief because the overall gain was too large to be held over.

In that example, Benito had £550,000 worth of property that originally cost £200,000, so a gain on transfer to his company of £350,000.

However, Benito's mortgages were £250,000, so the net value of his portfolio was only £300,000, (£550,000 - £250,000), and he could not therefore hold over the full gain as it exceeded the *net* value of the portfolio transferred in - £50,000 could not be held over, and was chargeable immediately.

Let's assume that Benito does not want to (or cannot) borrow more money to pay off his immediate CGT bill straight away, but would prefer to pay it off by instalments, over the next ten years. From a cost/benefit perspective, Benito reckons that the additional CGT cost over the next ten years will be 'worth it' if they can be funded out of the income tax he stands to save, if he incorporates his BTL business and therefore avoids the impending restriction of income tax relief for dwelling-related loans.

Instalment payments
The gain that Benito could not postpone was £50,000. Assuming Benito is already a higher rate (40%) taxpayer (using 2016/17 rates, etc.):

£50,000 - £11,100 annual exemption = £38,900, taxable at 28% (residential property) = £10,892

Each instalment payment will be £1,089 + the interest that will have accumulated to date on that repayment:

'Capital'	Year	Rate	Interest	Total
1,089	0	2.75%	-	1,089
1,089	1	2.75%	30	1,119
1,089	2	2.75%	60	1,149
1,089	3	2.75%	90	1,179
1,089	4	2.75%	120	1,209
1,089	5	2.75%	150	1,239
1,089	6	2.75%	180	1,269
1,089	7	2.75%	210	1,299
1,089	8	2.75%	240	1,329
1,089	9	2.75%	270	1,359
10,890			**1,350**	**12,238**

This equates to an *average* extra cost of £1,224, annually (£12,240 ÷ 10)

Income tax saving
To work out whether or not the extra cost is worthwhile, Benito needs to consider what the alternative cost will be in 'staying put', and paying the extra tax on disallowed mortgage interest. For the purposes of this exercise, Benito thinks it is worthwhile if the additional income tax due, if he were not to incorporate, were to be at least as much as the additional CGT he would have to pay over the next ten years. It is important to emphasise, however, that Benito is only saving money through

incorporation because the alternative is that much worse: he is unlikely to end up better off overall; rather he will not be as poorly off.

Benito's mortgages total £250,000 and he is paying 2.5%, interest only – equivalent to £6,250 in interest each year. We have already established that Benito is a 40% taxpayer, so the cost of this disallowed interest (once it is 100% disallowed by 2020/21) will be:

£6,250 @ (40% - 20%) = £1,250

Benito will suffer the disallowance of his interest cost at 40%, but will ordinarily get a basic rate 'credit' to set against his income tax liability, so his net tax cost is only 20%.

In other words, he would be paying an extra £1,250 in income tax by not incorporating, and only an extra £1,224 CGT by incorporating and suffering CGT by instalments over the next ten years.

In this example, it is a close-run comparison, but Benito will be slightly better off by incorporating over the next ten years – in essence, the CGT instalments are mathematically self-funding – and significantly better off after ten years, when he can properly 'enjoy' the benefit of the relative income tax saving.

20.5.3. Other Considerations

The exercise assumes that Benito is looking at incorporation only when BTL interest has been fully disallowed, so ignoring the 25% increments that apply from 2017/18 through to 2020/21.

The benefit of inflationary effects, etc. on paying something off over time have been ignored. It also assumes that the CGT annual exemption will be £11,100 when this happens. Perhaps most importantly, it assumes that the late payment interest rate will remain at 2.75% throughout.

Where the sums involved are significant, then it would be appropriate to consider discounting future payments to their 'net present value' (basically, that a commitment to pay £1,089 in nine years' time is better than a commitment to pay £1,089 today, thanks to inflation or whatever better use one can put the money to in that interval), and to consider the effect of an increase in interest rate.

20.5.4. Paying By Instalments Conclusion

The option to pay by instalments mean that, even where CGT is unavoidable on incorporation, it may be defrayed by up to a decade, and may therefore be significantly more manageable from a cashflow perspective. Depending on the amounts involved, the mathematical modelling may need to be much more precise than the simple illustration above – and there is always the risk, given the timeframe, that a new Chancellor – or a new government – will fundamentally change the relevant tax rules, for better or for worse.

21. Will A Property Management Company Save Me Tax?

<u>Consider the following case study:</u>

Say you own half a dozen properties, which produce gross rents of £60,000 a year, and a rental profit of £40,000 after expenses. Depending on your circumstances, you will be paying income tax at 40% on at least part of this profit – let's say, on £10,000 of it. You set up a company to manage the rentals. It does not own the properties – it charges you a fee for managing them, in the same way any other letting agency or estate agent might.

A typical "arm's length" property management fee is between 10% and 15% of the rents received, so if we take 15%, the company will charge you £9,000 for collecting your £60,000 rents. It will probably cost about £600 per year to run the company (accountant's fees, etc.).

Is it still worth it if the company is paying Corporation Tax (CT) at 20%?

If you are a basic rate taxpayer, the answer is no – the basic rate of income tax is 20% and CT is 19%. If you pay tax at 40%, is it still worth considering?

On the figures we used above, you save £3,600 income tax (£9,000 at 40%). The company pays CT at 19% on its profits of £8,400 (£9,000 fees, less £600 running costs), so the CT due is £1,596. Taking the running costs into account, the saving is now £1,404 (income tax saved = £3,600, less CT due £1,596 and running costs £600).

If you want to get the money out of the company, you have a choice; you can pay yourself dividends, but as a higher rate taxpayer your effective rate of income tax on these will be 32.5% on any amount above the £5,000 dividend allowance. (As from 6 Apr 18 the dividend allowance drops to £2,000.) Looking at our company again, it will have cash of £6,804 after paying its expenses and its CT. If you pay that out as a dividend, £559 income tax will be due (£5,000 @ 0% plus £1,720 @ 32.5%). (After 6 Apr 18 the dividend tax on £6,804 will be £1,561.30 (£2,000 @ 0% plus £4,804 @ 32.5%.)

If you liquidate the company after running it for at least one year, entrepreneurs' relief will mean that you pay capital gains tax @ 10%.

This all goes to show that although a property management company can still save you some money, it would be pretty borderline unless your rentals were approaching the £100,000 per year mark. Above those levels, however, it is still worth considering.

A word of warning – the strategy of liquidating a company to get the cash out free of tax is "provocative" (that is tax adviser's jargon for "it makes tax inspectors very cross") – you can't do it too often, and you **must** have advice from a tax specialist to avoid getting into trouble with the taxman! The Government have introduced new legislation to counteract 'phoenixism' - closing down a company, extracting the funds and paying a small amount of capital gains tax, and then starting a new company soon afterwards.

21.1. Draw Up Formal Contracts Between You and Your Company

Do not set up a company that manages your properties and just simply start paying money into it.

If you just go ahead and start making payments into your company, then the Inland Revenue could challenge you (if you are ever investigated) for making artificial transactions to avoid paying tax.

If you find that by using a property management company you will improve your tax position, then it is advisable to draw up a simple contract between you and your company.

Just drawing up a simple contract that outlines the services your company is providing to you will help to prevent such a challenge!

21.2. Beware Of Artificial Transactions!

Arthur Weller advises that you need to be careful and make sure that you are not creating artificial transactions that are aimed at avoiding tax.

In order words, the payments that you make to the company must be realistic and believable by the taxman.

For example, if you have a single property, then you can't pay £750 a month for property management–related charges. It is just not believable, and if you are ever investigated, then the taxman will for sure question whether you were making artificial transactions to avoid paying tax.

You must therefore pay an amount into a company that is believable and relates to the property. A good guide for you is to charge what a letting agent normally charges for their services. So, if your property management company charges you about 15% of your rental income, then this is both realistic and believable.

So, this means that

- for a rental income of £400pcm you can pay your company £60pcm;
- for rental income of £800pcm you can pay your company £120pcm;
- for rental income of £1,200pcm you can pay your company £180pcm.

Stamp Duty Land & Property Tax

22. Saving On Stamp Duty

In this section you will understand when you are liable to pay stamp duty.

22.1.   When Do Property Investors Pay Stamp Duty?

The Chancellor of the Exchequer announced a change in the stamp duty rates during his 2015 autumn statement. The following table provides details of the current rates of stamp duty for residential property which have become effective from 1st April 2016.

A new series of stamp duty rates have been introduced for second and subsequent residential properties, which will be effective for property investors.

Stamp Duty Rates

	First residential property	Second and subsequent residential properties – from 1 April 2016
When payment for the property is up to £40,000	Zero	Zero
When payment for the property is over £40,000, then the SDLT on any amount up to the first £125,000	Zero	3%
Next £125,000 (£125,001 to £250,000)	2%	5%
Next £675,000 (£250,001 to £925,000)	5%	8%
Next £575,000 (£925,001 to £1.5 million)	10%	13%
Remainder above £1.5m	12%	15%

The example that follow will assume that the second and subsequent residential properties stamp duty rate applies.

22.1.1.   Stamp Duty When Buying New Land Or Property

When purchasing land or property, you will be liable to pay stamp duty before you have completed the deal. Typically, the solicitor acting on your behalf in the transaction will include this tax liability in his final invoice to you.

> ### Stamp Duty Land Tax When Buying A Second Property
>
> Haleema buys a second property for £185,000.
>
> The rates of stamp duty will be as follows:
>
> | | | |
> |---|---|---|
> | The first £125,000 | - | 3% |
> | The next £60,000 | - | 5% |
>
> The means the total amount payable will be:
>
> | | | |
> |---|---|---|
> | The first £125,000 | - | £3,750 |
> | The next £60,000 | - | £3,000 (£60,000 * 0.05) |
>
> <u>Total Due:</u>   <u>£6,750</u>
>
> This means the total amount of stamp duty due is £6,750.

> ### Stamp Duty When Purchasing A Second Property
>
> Howard buys a buy-to-let property for £500,000.
>
> The rates of stamp duty will be as follows:
>
> | | | |
> |---|---|---|
> | The first £125,000 | - | 3% |
> | The next £125,000 | - | 5% |
> | The next £250,000 | - | 8% |
>
> The means the total amount payable will be:
>
> | | | |
> |---|---|---|
> | The first £125,000 | - | £3,750 |
> | The next £125,000 | - | £6,250 (£125,000 * 0.05) |
> | The next £250,000 | - | £20,000 (£250,000 * 0.08) |
>
> <u>Total Due:</u>   <u>£30,000</u>
>
> This means the total amount of stamp duty due is £30,000.

22.1.2.   Stamp Duty When Transferring A Property

What a lot of investors fail to realise is that if you transfer ownership of a property to another party (including husband/wife), then stamp duty will be liable if the property is mortgaged and the mortgage amount being transferred is over £40,000.

If the property is not mortgaged and ownership is being gifted, then there is no stamp duty liability.

Stamp Duty When Transferring A Second Property

This case study continues from the previous case study, where Howard has now purchased his property and already incurred a charge of £30,000 in stamp duty.

Two years after the purchase, he marries his long-term girlfriend Betty. He decides to move the property into joint names, where they will have equal 50:50 ownership of the property.

The outstanding amount on the mortgage at the time of transfer is £200,000. By transferring the mortgage into joint names, Betty will liable to pay any additional stamp duty tax as follows on her share of £100,000 of the mortgage:

The first £100,000   -   3%

The means the total amount payable will be:

The first £100,000   -   £3,000

                 Total Due: £3,000

This means the total amount of stamp duty due is £3,000.

However in the Autumn 2017 Budget the Government announced that as from 22 November 2017 the higher rate of SDLT will not apply to transfers between husband and wife.

Other Property Investment Strategies

23. Tax-Free Income For Renting Out Part Of Your Home

In this section you will learn about generous annual tax-free savings that are available if you rent out part of your main home.

This tax relief is known as the **rent-a-room** relief.

23.1.   What Is The Rent-A-Room Relief?

If you decide to let a room in your main residence, you can receive a rental income of up to £7,500 and have no tax liability[3]. This new rate has become effective from 6th April 2016.

Prior to this the rate was £4,250.

In order to claim this allowance, the property must satisfy the following conditions:

a)   you must also live in the property as your main home, at the same time as the tenant, for at least part of the letting period in each tax year;

b)   the room you are letting out must be fully furnished.

If you claim the rent-a-room relief, then it is not possible to claim any expenditure that you have incurred with regards to the letting.

This is a very common strategy for those people who have houses that are too large for their needs. For example, if your children have left home, then you may decide to rent the room they lived in for an additional tax-free income.

Rent-a-Room Relief (1)

Bill and Mary have a three-bedroom detached house. They are both higher-rate taxpayers.

Their daughter Louise leaves home and moves in with her long-term boyfriend, so they decide to let her room out to a local teacher.

They receive an annual rental income of £4,000 per annum.

There is no tax liability on this income as it is below the £7,500 threshold value.

If the income received is greater than the annual allowance, then tax is liable on the amount above this value.

---

[3] All that is necessary is to tick the rent-a-room box at the beginning of the land and property page of the tax return.

Rent-a-Room Relief (2)

Howard is a bachelor but lives in a luxury five-bedroom detached house on the outskirts of London. He is also a higher-rate taxpayer.

He decides to let a room to a newly graduated doctor for £8,500 per annum.

Howard will have no tax liability on the first £7,500. However, he will be liable to pay tax on the remaining £1,000 of income at 40%. This means that he will be liable to pay £400 in tax.

If you decide to let a room in your main residence and claim the relief, then you must inform HMRC. This is regardless of whether you will have a tax liability.

If you do not inform HMRC, then you will be taxed as though you are running a normal property-letting business, where your expenses will be deducted from any rental income you receive.

23.2.   Choosing Not to Use The Relief

Consider not using the relief if you have high income and also high expenses.

If you are letting a room in your property, then it is not necessary that you claim the relief. As mentioned in the previous section, you will be taxed as a normal property-letting business if you do not inform HMRC that you want to use the relief.

Generally speaking, if your rental income is going to be significantly greater than £7,500, then it may not be beneficial to use the relief.

The following two case studies illustrate typical scenarios when it is beneficial to use each method.

When it is Beneficial to Use the Rent-a-Room Relief

John is a higher-rate taxpayer and lets out a room in his property for £10,000 per annum. His expenses are £1,000.

Tax liability if rent-a-room relief is *not* claimed
If rent-a-room relief is not claimed, then he has a taxable income of £9,000 (i.e., £10,000 − £1,000).

This means that his tax liability is calculated as follows:
        40% × £9,000 = **£3,600**

Tax liability if rent-a-room relief *is* claimed
If rent-a-room relief is claimed, then he has a taxable income of £2,500 (i.e.,

£10,000 − £7,500).

This means that his tax liability is calculated as follows:
    40% × £2,500 = **£1,000**

As you can see from the above case study, it is beneficial for John to claim the rent-a-room relief. This is because by claiming it, John will pay **£2,600** less in tax on an annual basis. Over a 10-year period, this is **£26,000** in tax savings.

When it is NOT Beneficial to Use the Rent-a-Room Relief

Lisa is a higher-rate taxpayer and lets out a room in her property for £13,000 per annum. Her expenses are £9,000 per annum.

Tax liability if rent-a-room relief is *not* claimed
If rent-a-room relief is not claimed, then she has a taxable income of £4,000 (i.e., £13,000 − £9,000).

This means that her tax liability is calculated as follows:
    40% × £4,000 = **£1,600**

Tax liability if rent-a-room relief *is* claimed
If rent-a-room relief is claimed, then she has a taxable income of £4,500 (i.e., £13,000 − £7,500).

This means that her tax liability is calculated as follows:
    40% × £5,500 = **£2,200**

As you can see from the above case study, it is beneficial for Lisa *not* to use the rent-a-room relief. This is because by claiming it, Lisa will pay **£600** less in tax on an annual basis. Over a 10-year period, this is **£6,000** in tax savings.

> It is possible to switch between the 'Rent-a-Room' allowance and the "strict" method from year to year if you wish.

23.3.   Renting Out In Joint Ownership

The exemption limit of £7,500 is reduced to £3,750 if during the tax year to April 5, someone else received income from letting accommodation in the same property.

This is likely to occur if you own a property in a partnership.

24. Generous Tax Breaks For Holiday Lets

In this section you will become familiar with the tax benefits associated with those who provide holiday lets.

There have been considerable changes to the Furnished Holiday Lettings (FHL) rules recently. First, we start with the old rules:

24.1.   Qualifying Criteria For A Holiday Let

If you let a property in a popular holiday location, e.g., the south coast, then you could well be operating a holiday lettings business. This is especially the case if your target market is people visiting and staying in your property for short periods of time.

In order to qualify your property as a holiday let, it must be fully furnished; that is, anyone moving into the property must be able to live out of the property without having to buy any additional furniture/furnishings.

It must also satisfy the following three conditions:

- the property must be available to let to the public on a commercial basis for at least 140 days;

- the property must be let for at least 70 days;

- let for periods of longer-term occupation (more than 31 consecutive days) for not more than 155 days during the year.

Income tax on a holiday let is charged in the same way as if you are operating a normal lettings business, where tax will be liable on any rental profits less expenses.

Holiday Lets

John buys a three-bedroom property in Bournemouth. His investment strategy is to rent the property in the summer periods to visiting holiday makers.

He offers the property for £250 per week.

Over the financial year, it is let for 35 weeks, which means that he has received a total rental income of £8,750. His expenses are £2,750.

This means that he is liable to pay tax on the £6,000 profit.

24.2.   Three Generous Tax Benefits Associated With Holiday Lets

Operating a holiday letting business has three *significant* tax benefits. These are detailed below.

24.2.1.   Offsetting losses against other income

If you are unfortunate enough to make a loss in your holiday lettings business, then the loss is treated as a trading loss and can be offset against any other source of income that you have, in the same way as trading losses.

Holiday Lets – Offsetting Losses

Kiran buys a property for the purpose of holiday letting for £130,000 in 1995.

Her first year of letting is very tough and she makes a £2,500 rental loss.

However, because she is employed with a salary of £35,000, she is able to offset the loss against this income.

In other words, she pays less tax on her employment income.

24.2.2.   Re-investment Of Capital Gains

If you decide to sell your holiday let and make a capital gain, then the sale proceeds can be re-invested into another qualifying asset, thus avoiding any immediate capital gains tax liability. This therefore means that you will not liable to pay any capital gains tax until you dispose of the asset you have re-invested in.

However, you can continue selling and re-investing the sale proceeds. By doing this, you will continue to defer any tax liability until the point at which you stop re-investing the sales proceeds.

Holiday Lets – Re-investment of Capital Gains

Continuing from the previous example.

Kiran sells her property 5 years later for £230,000, thus meaning she has made a profit of £100,000.

She buys another 'holiday let' property in the same tax year by re-investing the sale proceeds and therefore is able to defer any CGT liability.

24.2.3.   FHL – New Rules

- From 2009 FHL in the European Economic Area (EEA) qualified for the special rules available to FHL's in the UK, and from 2011 this became statutory.
- From 2011-12 the accommodation must be available to the public as holiday accommodation for at least 210 days, and actually let as such for at least 105 of those days.

- From April 2011 income from an FHL business (either in the UK or EEA) has to be computed separately from other property business income (again either in the UK or EEA) for the purposes of capital allowances, loss relief and relevant earnings for pension contributions.

- Trade loss reliefs used to be available, but from April 2011 loss relief is not available against general income. Losses can, therefore, only be set against income from the same UK or EEA FHL business.

- The rules restricting interest relief for residential landlords do not apply to FHL's.

25. Tax Implications When Converting Properties Into Flats

Many a property developer has spotted the potential of buying a large property and converting it into flats in order to maximise profit. However, converting a property into flats for financial gain is not the sole preserve of the property developer.

A landlord may decide to convert a property into flats to maximise both rental income in the short term and profit on sale in the longer term. Likewise, a person may decide to convert a former family home into flats to realise the maximum possible gain on disposal. However, as is often the case, the tax implications will vary depending on the circumstances.

25.1. Scenario 1

A developer buys up a large house in a poor state of repair for £400,000. He spends a further £200,000 converting into four flats. The work takes six months. Once complete, the flats are sold for £250,000 each.

The nature of a property developer's trade is to develop properties for profit. As in this scenario the motive is to make a profit rather than to buy the property as an investment, any profit on sale is charged to income tax as a trading profit rather than to capital gains tax. The trading profit would be computed according to normal rules and the profit on this development (£400,000) would be taken into account in computing the developer's trading profits for the period in question.

As the developer is trading, capital gains tax (CGT) is not in point. Consequently, there is no CGT to pay when the flats are sold.

25.2. Scenario 2

A landlord has a number of properties that he lets out. He has owned a large property for a number of years which has been let out as a single dwelling. He decides to convert the property into flats. He then lets the flats for a further couple of years before selling them.

The landlord will be subject to CGT on any gain made from the sale of the flats. As the flats have always been let and have never been the landlord's main residence, neither private residence relief or letting relief are in point.

For the purposes of illustration, it is assumed that the landlord originally bought the house in 2005 for £300,000 and let it as a single unit until June 2009, when he converted the property into three flats. The conversion costs were £150,000. Each flat has two bedrooms and is approximately the same size.

The work was completed in November 2009 and the flats were again let until January 2011, when they were put on the market. Flat 1 sold in February 2011 for £220,000, Flat 2 also sold in February 2011 but for £230,000, and Flat 3 sold in March 2011 for £215,000. It is assumed that in each case the costs of sale are £2,000.

The gains on disposal are as follows:

Flat 1

Proceeds		£220,000
Less: cost of original property (1/3 x £300,000)	£100,000	
Conversion costs (1/3 x £150,000)	£50,000	
		(£150,000)
		£70,000
Less: costs of disposal		(£2,000)
Gain on sale		£68,000

Flat 2

Proceeds		£230,000
Less: cost of original property (1/3 x £300,000)	£100,000	
Conversion costs (1/3 x £150,000)	£50,000	
		(£150,000)
		£80,000
Less: costs of disposal		(£2,000)
Gain on sale		£78,000

Flat 3

Proceeds		£215,000
Less: cost of original property (1/3 x £300,000)	£100,000	
Conversion costs (1/3 x £150,000)	£50,000	
		(£150,000)
		£65,000
Less: costs of disposal		(£2,000)
Gain on sale		£63,000

The total gains on the sale of the flats (£209,000) will be taken into account in computing the landlord's net chargeable gains for 2010/11 and charged to CGT at the appropriate rate.

25.3. Scenario 3

After his children have grown up, a homeowner decides to convert his property into flats prior to sale to maximise the profit on sale. The flats are sold as soon as the work is complete.

For the purposes of illustration, it is assumed that the property was purchased in 1990 for £100,000. It was lived in as the taxpayer's main residence until June 2010, at which time work began to convert the property into three flats. The work was completed in November 2010, and the flats were sold in January 2011 for £275,000 each. The conversion work cost £180,000.

At first sight, it may seem that the entire gain is covered by private residence relief as it had been the taxpayer's home throughout the period of ownership. However, there is a trap that will catch the unwary. This is because private residence relief is denied in respect of a gain in so far that it is attributable to any expenditure that is incurred after the beginning of a period of ownership that is incurred wholly or partly for the purposes of realising a gain.

Broadly, the provisions work to deny private residence relief in relation to that portion of the gain that is attributable to the expenditure incurred in order to realise a higher profit. It is therefore necessary to obtain a valuation of the house assuming the work had not been carried out and it was sold as a single dwelling. In this way, it is possible to establish the additional profit attributable to the conversion work.

In the above example, it is assumed that had the property been sold as the original family home it would have fetched £600,000. By converting it into flats, the sale proceeds increased to £825,000 (3 x £275,000). The cost attributable to the additional proceeds of £225,000 (i.e. £825,000 - £600,000) was the conversion expenditure of £180,000. This expenditure effectively generated an additional gain of £45,000 (£225,000 - £180,000). The development gain does not qualify for private residence relief.

The computation of the gain is therefore as follows:

	Total Gain £	Exempt Gain £	Non-Exempt Gain £
Proceeds	825,000	600,000	225,000
Less: cost of property	(100,000)	(100,000)	
cost of extension	(180,000)		(180,000)
GAIN	545,000	500,000	45,000

The non-exempt gain is reduced by the taxpayer's annual allowance to the extent that this remains available and charged to CGT at the appropriate rate.

25.4. Scenario 4

A homeowner decides that her house is too big for her. She converts it into two flats, one of which she sells. She continues to live in the remaining flat.

The property was purchased in 2000 for £325,000. In 2010, the property was converted into two flats. The conversion work was completed in May 2010. One flat was sold in June 2010 for £275,000. The conversion costs were £40,000. At that date, the value of the unconverted house was £500,000 and the value of the flat retained was £350,000.

The combined value of the two flats at the date the flat was sold was £625,000. This is £125,000 more than the value of the unconverted property at that date. The conversion costs are £40,000, giving rise to a gain attributable to conversion of £85,000.

This gain is not covered by the private residence exemption. However, it must be attributed between the flats to ascertain the amount that comes into charge in respect of the sale of the first flat. This is done simply on an apportionment basis by reference to the relative values of each property on the date that the first flat was sold.

The non-exempt gain attributable to the flat sold is therefore:

£275,000/£625,000 x £85,000 = £37,400.

The remainder of the gain attributable to the first flat is covered by private residence relief.

The non-exempt gain (as reduced by any allowable losses and the annual exemption to the extent that it remains available) is charged to CGT at the appropriate rate (18% or 28% depending on whether the taxpayer is a higher rate taxpayer).

The balance of the non-exempt gain will come into charge on the eventual sale of the flat which has become the taxpayer's home.

How To Slash Your Property Capital Gains Tax

26. Understanding Capital Gains Tax (CGT)

Before we look at the different ways to cut your capital gains tax saving strategies, it is important to understand what is meant by the term **capital gains tax (CGT)** and when property investors are liable to pay it.

In this section you will become familiar with CGT and how it is calculated when you decide to sell your property.

26.1.   When You Are Liable to Pay CGT

A property investor is likely to incur a CGT liability in the following two situations:

a)   when a property is sold at a higher price than for which it was purchased;

b)   when a property, or part of a property, is transferred to a non-spouse.

Properties and other assets can be transferred between husband and wife freely, without triggering a CGT liability.

Both of the above situations are illustrated in the following case studies.

CGT Liability When Selling a Property

Maria purchases a buy-to-let property in January 1998 for £100,000. She rents it out for five years and then sells it for £210,000.

This means that she has made a capital gain of £110,000, upon which she is liable to pay CGT.

CGT Liability When Transferring a Property

Maria purchases a buy-to-let property in January 1998 for £100,000. She rents it out for five years and then gifts the property to her mother.

She receives no payment from her mother for the property.

Although Maria has received no payment for the property, she is treated as having transferred the property to her mother at 'market value,' which is £210,000. Therefore, again, Maria is liable to pay CGT on the £110,000 profit.

Property dealers/traders are not liable to pay CGT. When they sell a property, the profit is classed as a dealing profit, and therefore they are liable to pay **income tax** on the profits.

26.2.   Recent History And Changes To The CGT Rate

October 2007
In the October 2007 pre-budget report, Chancellor Alistair Darling announced that a flat rate CGT rate of 18% would be introduced from April 6th, 2008.

March 2008
The announcement in the October 2007 pre-budget report was confirmed in the March 2008 budget and became effective from 6th April 2008.

What this meant was that any property sold from 6th April 2008 would only pay a flat rate capital gains tax of 18%, regardless of the size of profit.

It was no surprise that a number of commentators referred to the March 2008 budget as a budget for the **property investor!**

June 22nd, 2010
In the 22 June 2010 Budget Chancellor George Osborne announced new CGT rates. Capital gains made on disposals from 23 June 2010 onwards are added to the taxpayer's other income.

Any gains falling below the higher rate threshold are taxed at 18%. Any gains falling above the threshold are taxed at 28%.

Trusts pay capital gains tax at only one rate – 28%.

In the March 2016 budget the Chancellor reduced the rates of capital gains tax to 20% for a higher rate taxpayer, and 10% for a basic rate taxpayer. However, a capital gain on the sale of a residential property will still be subject to the old rates of 28% and 18%.

The Government has now introduced that as from April 2020 the payment window for gains on residential property will be 30 days from completion.

26.3.   How Your CGT Bill Is Calculated

Calculating the tax liability on the sale or transfer of a property is not easy.

Given the property price increases over the past few years alone, investors are sitting on significant capital gains.

It is important to realise that a number of reliefs and strategies are available to reduce any CGT liability you may have. The most significant of these are detailed in the remainder of this guide.

However, listed in the table below are the typical reliefs/reductions that can be claimed when a property is sold/transferred.

If applicable, these can be offset against the capital gain made on the property and can be used to significantly reduce any tax liability.

Relief/Reduction	Description
Buying and Selling Costs	Typical purchase costs include • solicitor' fees; • estate agency fees • survey costs; • cost of searches, e.g., land, mining, etc. • stamp duty land tax Typical selling costs include • estate agency fees; • solicitor' fees; • redemption penalties, etc. See section 34.3 for further details.
Capital Costs	If you have incurred costs of a capital nature, then these can also be offset. A capital cost is one that has increased the price of the property. Examples of capital costs include the building of conservatories, additional bedrooms, loft conversions, garage conversions, etc.
Indexation Relief	This relief was available for qualifying for property that was sold before April 6th, 2008.
Private Residence Relief	This relief is based on the period that the property was classed as your PPR. See sections 27, 32 & 33 for further details.
Private Letting Relief	This relief is a relief for a property that was at one time your private residence that can reduce your capital gain by up to an additional £40,000. It was

	available up until 5th April 2020. See section 31 for further details.
Allowable Losses	If you have incurred capital losses, then these can be offset against any capital gain made when you dispose of your property. See section 34.2 for further details.
Taper Relief	This relief was introduced in April 1998 and was a replacement for indexation relief. However, it can only be claimed for property sold before 6th April 2008.
Personal CGT Allowance	For the 2020-21 tax year it is £12,300. See section 34.1 for further details.

28. Reporting And Tax Payment Changes From 6th April 2020

From a capital gains tax (CGT) perspective, making a gain on a property that has always been the owner's only or main residence is a 'good thing' as the gain can be enjoyed free of tax, even if the owner jumps off the property ladder following the sale.

However, when it comes to gains on residential property where full private residence relief is not available, the tax regime is increasingly punitive; not only does a higher rate of tax apply to residential property gains than other gains (with the exception of carried interest), from April 2020 the timescale for reporting such gains to HMRC and paying the associated tax is significantly reduced.

28.1. When May A Residential Property Gain Arise?

Private residence relief applies to shelter a property that has been the owner's only or main residence throughout the period of ownership. The availability of the final period exemption and lettings relief may mean even where a property has not always been the only or main residence, any gain can still be enjoyed free of CGT.

However, where a property has never been the only or main residence, or where relief is not available in full, a chargeable gain will arise. If it is not offset by allowable losses or covered by the annual exempt amount, CGT will be payable.

Gains made on the sale of investment properties (e.g. buy-to-let investments and second homes such as holiday homes) may give rise to a residential property gain on which CGT is payable.

The announced curtailment of lettings relief and the reduction in the final period exemption will bring more property sales within the CGT net from 6 April 2020 onwards, increasing the number of taxpayers who will be affected by the new rules.

28.2. Higher Tax Rates For Residential Property Gains

Not all gains are equal, and higher rates of CGT apply to residential property gains (and carried interest).

The rate at which CGT is payable depends on whether total income and gains exceed the basic rate limit (which was £37,500 for 2019/20). Up to this limit, residential gains are taxed at 18% (compared to 10% for other gains); thereafter, the tax rate is 28% (compared to 20% for other gains).

28.3. Reporting Pre-6 April 2020 Residential Property Gains

Chargeable residential property gains arising prior to 6 April 2020 are reported with other gains arising in the tax year to HMRC on the CGT pages of the self-assessment return. This must be filed by 31 January after the end of the tax year to which it relates.

Gains arising in the 2019/20 tax year, including any chargeable residential property gains, must normally be notified to HMRC by 31 January 2021.

One CGT bill
Prior to 6 April 2020, the total CGT liability for the year, reflecting all chargeable gains and allowable losses (including any brought forward losses), and allowing for the annual exempt amount, is worked out as part of the self-assessment for the year. Any CGT for the year must be paid by 31 January after the end of the tax year. It is not necessary to deal with any chargeable residential property gains separately; everything goes into the pot.

This gives a lag of between nearly nine and nearly 22 months between realising the gains and reporting it to HMRC and paying the tax, depending on when in the tax year the gain arose.

28.4.   New Rules From 6 April 2020

Where a residential property gain arises on a direct disposal of UK land or property by a UK resident on or after 6 April 2020, a new return must be completed and filed with HMRC within 30 days of the date of the disposal.

A return is only required where a gain is made; no return is needed if (for example) a second home or an investment property is sold at a loss. Likewise, a return is not required if the gain is entirely sheltered by private residence relief (including, where applicable, the final period exemption and lettings relief). Nor is a return required for disposals between spouses and civil partners on a no gain/no loss basis, disposals by a charity or of a pension scheme investment, or where the disposal in question is the grant of a lease at arm's length for no premium.

Once made, the return can be amended within a 12-month window, but only in respect of events that had arisen at the time the disposal was made.

28.5.   Requirement To Make A Payment On Account

From 6 April 2020, a new CGT payment window applies in respect of UK residential property gains realised by a UK resident. Where such a gain is made on or after that date, a payment on account of the CGT due on that disposal must be paid within 30 days of the disposal – matching the deadline for filing the associated return.

This is considerably earlier than for pre-April 2020 gains, in respect of which the normal CGT deadline of 31 January after the end of the tax year applies. The change creates an anomaly such that CGT on residential gains arising in the period from 6 April 2020 to 31 December 2020 will be due before those arising in 2019/20.

28.6.   Calculating The Payment On Account

In working out the CGT on post-6 April 2020 residential property gains, the annual exempt amount can be taken into account, as can any allowable losses brought forward or realised prior to the disposal.

However, losses arising after the disposal cannot be taken into account, even if these are realised in the 30-day window for filing the return and making the payment on account.

28.7.   Finalising The Position

In much the same way as payments on account for income tax purposes are taken into account in finalising the tax bill under self-assessment, payments made on account will be reflected in determining the overall liability for the tax year under the self-assessment position. The total CGT liability for the year will calculated (initially at least) through the self-assessment system reflecting all gains and losses in the year.

If the final bill is more than the payment made on account (e.g. because non-residential gains have also arisen in the tax year), the excess must be paid by 31 January after the end of the tax year. In the event that the final bill for the tax year is less (e.g. because losses have been realised after the residential property gain) a refund of the excess can be claimed once the self-assessment return has been filed.

Sale Of Holiday Home

Imogen completes on the sale of her holiday home on 10 April 2020, realising a gain of £75,000. She has made no other disposals at this point in the 2020/21 tax year. She is a higher rate taxpayer.

In working out the payment on account, Imogen can take her annual exempt amount for 2020/21 into account. The chargeable gain is, therefore, £62,700 (i.e. £75,000 - £12,300) on which CGT of 28% (i.e. £17,556) must be paid by 10 May 2020. The associated return must be filed by the same date.

In August 2020, Imogen sells some shares, realising a loss of £4,600. She makes no other disposals in 2020/21.

For 2020/21, she realises net gains of £70,400 (£75,000 - £4,600), leaving her with chargeable gains of £58,100 after deducting her annual exempt amount of £12,300, on which the overall CGT liability is £16,268. However, Imogen has already made a payment on account of £17,556 and is, therefore, due a refund of £1,288.

---

29. Private Residence Relief (PPR)

In this section you will become familiar with the extremely powerful **private residence relief**.

This allowance on its own can wipe out tens or even hundreds of thousands of pounds off your chargeable capital gains.

29.1.   What Is Private Residence Relief?

This relief is available to you if you have lived in a property that has been classed as your **main residence** for a period of time.

This relief is not available to you if you are a property dealer and purchased a property with the sole intention of making a dealing profit, i.e., you did not make it your main residence.

The technical name for a person's main residence is **principle private residence (PPR)**.

> If you have lived in a property that has been your PPR, then you are not liable to pay any capital gains tax on the price appreciation that is attributed to the period when you lived in the property.

There are two types of residence relief that are available, and both are described and illustrated in the following two sections.

29.1.1.   Full Residence Relief

If the property has been classed as your PPR throughout your period of ownership, then you can claim **full residence relief**.

If you can claim full residence relief, then this means that you will have no CGT liability. This is regardless of the capital profit you have made on the property.

Every homeowner who has occupied their property since the first day of ownership up until the time of sale is entitled to use this relief.

Full Residence Relief

Alex buys his first home in May 1990 for £65,000. He lives in it from the day of purchase up until the day he sells it in June 2001. The selling price is £150,000, which means that he has made a capital profit of £85,000. He is not liable to pay any tax on this profit as he is able to claim full residence relief because the property was his main residence during his period of ownership.

29.1.2. Partial Residence Relief

You are able to claim **partial residence relief** if your property has been your main residence for a period of time but not for the whole period of ownership.

If you are claiming partial residence relief, then the amount of relief you can claim is determined by dividing the periods when the property was classed as your PPR by the total periods of ownership.

For example, if you purchased a property, let it out for 7 years and then lived in it for three years before selling it then you will be able to claim 3/10 partial residence relief. This is because you owned the property for 10 years, but it was your main residence for three of those years.

You are most likely to claim partial residence relief if

- you have a second home (see section 33 for more details on how you can legitimately reduce your tax liability by nominating your main residence);

- you are a property investor who has let a property after having previously lived in it.

29.2. How Long In A Property Before It Can Be Classed As My PPR?

This is one of the most commonly asked tax questions.

The reason for the popularity of this question is because if you can prove that a property was genuinely your PPR, you can make use of some very generous tax reliefs. You will see in the following strategies exactly how you can use these reliefs to your advantage to reduce or even wipe out any tax liability.

HMRC have not given any specific guidance as to how long you need to live in a property before you can claim that it has been your principle private residence.

However, as a general rule of thumb, you should try to make it your permanent residence for at least one year, i.e., 12 months.

The longer you live in a property, the better chance you have of claiming residence relief.

HMRC are not necessarily interested in how long you lived in the property. They are *much more* interested in whether the property really was your home and whether you *really* did live in the property!

If you want to claim this relief, here are some pointers that will help you to convince the taxman that a property genuinely was your private residence.

a) Have utility and other bills in your own name at the property address.

Typical bills will include
  i. gas bills;
  ii. water rates;

      iii.   electricity supply bills;

      iv.   council tax bills;

      v.   TV licence, etc.

b) Make the property address your voting address on the electoral register.

c) Be able to demonstrate that you bought furniture and furnishings for the property. Keep receipts and prove that bulky furniture was delivered to the property address.

d) Have all bank statements delivered to the property address.

By following the above guidelines, you will be in a good position to convince the taxman that a property was genuinely your home.

29.3.   More Insight Into What Makes A PPR

A case heard by the Tax Tribunal (AJ Clarke v HMRC) has shed more light on what it takes to make a property your 'main residence' and thus exempt from capital gains tax (CGT).

Mr Clarke lived with his wife and children at Oaks Farm. His marriage was failing and he wanted to get his children away from his wife's influence. He bought 60 Nayland Road in July 2002 and moved in with his children. He had used a short term loan to buy it and needed to raise money to pay off the loan, so he obtained planning permission to build another property (58a) in the garden of No 60.

He put No 60 on the market in December 2002, only 5 months after buying it, and it sold in March 2003. He moved in with his mother while 58a was completed, and was able to occupy it in July 2003.

In July 2005, he had to move back to Oaks Farm, as his (now divorced) wife had attempted suicide and he felt he had to be there. Number 58a was put on the market and sold in November 2005.

HMRC argued that neither of the Nayland Road properties had ever been his main residence and were thus not exempt from CGT. They pointed out that he had not notified anyone of his changes of address, and correspondence for him continued to be sent to him at Oaks Farm, where he had an office from which he ran his business.

They also argued that the use of the short term loan to buy No 60 indicated that he bought it with the intention of selling it and developing another property in the garden – which of course is what he had in fact done.

Although HMRC grudgingly accepted that Mr Clarke had in fact resided at both of the Nayland Road properties, they said that his residence in both of them was merely a temporary measure and not intended to be the start of a new 'permanent home' – an expression that does not appear in the legislation, but one HMRC are fond of using in these disputes.

Mr Clarke could have made life much easier for himself if he had written to HMRC within two years of moving into No 60, nominating it as his main residence, and then done the same again when he moved into No 58a, but he had not done so within the two year time limit, so the question of which property was his main residence had to be decided on the facts.

Normally, a married couple can only have one main residence between them. The case report does not make it clear, but I assume that HMRC accepted that they were permanently separated at the time Mr Clarke bought No 60, so that potentially Mr Clarke could have a main residence of his own.

If Mr Clarke had come to me for advice, I would probably have said he had a good case as far as No 58a was concerned, as he had lived there for a couple of years, but that HMRC would probably win the argument on No 60, given how he had financed the purchase and how quickly he had put it on the market.

In fact, the Tribunal accepted that both 60 and 58a had been Mr Clarke's main residence while he occupied them, and so the gains on the sales were exempt from CGT.

They based their decision on the fact that they accepted Mr Clarke's evidence of what he had intended at the time he bought No 60 (to live there and to sell part of the land to repay the loan – the idea of building 58a had been suggested to him later by his business partner).

29.3.1. Practical Tip

The above case makes it clear that your intention when buying and moving into a property is the crucial factor in deciding whether it becomes your main residence, even if events subsequently lead you to change your mind.

29.4. Private Residence CGT Exemption - How To Lose It!

The capital gains tax (CGT) legislation which provides for relief on the disposal of a private residence includes a provision (in TCGA 1992, s 224(3)) which appears to deny the normal exemption for capital gains on a 'main residence' if you hoped to sell it at a profit when you bought it.

At the first reading, section 224 (3) seems to do away with almost all the CGT exemption. It says the main residence exemption:

"...shall not apply in relation to a gain if the acquisition of, or of the interest in, the dwelling-house or the part of a dwelling-house was made wholly or partly for the purpose of realising a gain from the disposal of it, and shall not apply in relation to a gain so far as attributable to any expenditure which was incurred after the beginning of the period of ownership and was incurred wholly or partly for the purpose of realising a gain from the disposal" (emphasis added).

Notice those two uses of 'or partly'- most of us hope to sell our homes at a profit one day, and adverts for home improvements like conservatories often make the point that this will increase the value of the property concerned. So are we all doomed to pay tax when we sell our homes? Fortunately, HMRC's Capital Gains manual instructs its staff to behave reasonably and not use the legislation in cases like these:

"It would be unreasonable and restrictive to apply the legislation in this way. The subsection should only be taken to apply when the primary purpose of the acquisition, or of the expenditure, was an early disposal at a profit" (CG65210).

HMRC generally use the legislation in three situations:

1. Quasi property development

It is difficult for HMRC to establish that someone who buys a run-down house, does it up, and then sells it in a short period of time is trading as a property developer if he genuinely lives in the property while he does so, and he has no other residence at the time, but they may use section 224(3) to charge CGT on the profit made.

2. Leasehold Enfranchisement

Tenants under a lease may get the opportunity to buy the freehold from their landlord. This is generally a sensible investment, but if you then sell the freehold shortly afterwards, you may find section 224(3) rears its head, as far as the gain attributable to the freehold is concerned.

3. Extensions and conversions

A house divided into flats will often sell for more than the same house undivided. If you do this (or build an extension) shortly before sale, then some of the gain may not be exempt.

4. Calculating the lost exemption

Except in the case of the 'property developer', it is not all of the gain that is taxed; it is only the part relating to the offending expenditure. This involves a valuation exercise.

For example, imagine a house converted into three flats and immediately sold. Each flat sells for £150,000, whereas the unconverted house would have sold for £350,000. The conversion work cost £50,000. The taxable gain is as follows:

Sale proceeds of three flats at £150,000 each	£450,000
Estimate of sale proceeds of unconverted house	(£350,000)
Gain attributable to conversion	£100,000
Less cost of conversion	(£50,000)
Taxable gain	£50,000

The longer the period between the expenditure and the sale, the less risk there is of section 224(3) being trotted out, especially if you can show another reason for the expenditure (an extension for a growing family, for example).

29.5. Private Residence Relief – When Relief May Be Restricted

No capital gains tax liability arises where a person sells his or her home provided that the property has been his or only or main residence throughout the period of ownership, except for all or any part of the last 18 months of ownership. If this condition is not met, principal private residence (PPR) relief generally applies to that fraction of the gain that related to the period for which the property was the taxpayer's only or main residence, including the last 18 months of ownership, divided by the length of ownership.

However, relief may be restricted where part of the property is used for the purposes of a trade, profession or vocation, or where there is a change in the part that is occupied as the individual's residence, or where the property was acquired wholly or partly for the purposes of realising a gain from its disposal. For sales after 5 April 2020, this final period exemption of 18 months is reduced to 9 months.

29.5.1. Restriction 1 – Use For Purpose Of A Trade, Business Profession Or Vocation

By virtue of TCGA 1992, s 224(1), where a gain arises on all or part of a dwelling house, part of which is used exclusively for the purposes of a trade or business, or a profession or vocation, the gain must be apportioned between the part used as a main residence and the part used for the trade, business, profession or vocation. PPR is not available in respect of the portion of the gain that relates to the part of the dwelling house used exclusively for the purposes of the trade, profession or vocation.

It should be noted that the exclusion from PPR relief applies only to any part of the property which is used exclusively for the purposes of the trade, business, profession or vocation. Consequently, relief is not lost in relation to a room that is used for both business and private purposes. In their Capital Gains manual, HMRC cite the example of the kitchen in a small guest house which is used equally to provide meals for the guests and also to provide meals for the resident owner. As the kitchen is not used exclusively for the purposes of the trade, there is no restriction in the availability of PPR.

In a case where a part of the property is used exclusively for the purposes of a trade, business, profession or vocation, the gain must be apportioned between the residential and non-residential parts. The legislation does not provide how the apportionment must be made, and this must be determined by reference to the facts of the particular case.

Some guidance as to HMRC's approach to the apportionment calculation can be found in their Capital Gains manual. Their willingness to accept a simple apportionment based, for example, on the number of rooms used for each purposes, will depend on the tax at stake. HMRC note in their Capital Gains Tax manual (at CG64670) that in a mixed property, such as a pub with residential accommodation above, the business part would be expected to be of greater value than the residential value. Consequently, an apportionment based solely on the number of rooms or the floor area attributable to residential and non-residential use could produce an excessive amount of relief. HMRC advise their inspectors to seek a valuation from the Valuation Office Agency if an apportionment appears to be unduly weighted in favour of the residential accommodation. However, they also state that in small cases any reasonable apportionment will be accepted.

It should also be noted that HMRC do not accept computations based on taking the value of the residential accommodation in isolation and deducting it from the consideration to determine the proportion attracting relief, as this is likely to produce excessive relief.

> **Apportioning The Gain For PPR Purposes**
>
> Holly runs a small guest house, in which she also lives as her main residence. The property comprises twelve rooms, of which four are used exclusively for the purposes of her business. In July 2016, she sells the property for £900,000. She originally purchased the property in 1990 for £300,000. On sale she realises a gain of £600,000.
>
> On a simple apportionment by reference to the number of rooms, two-thirds (i.e. 8/12) of the gain would qualify for PPR relief, leaving one-third (£200,000) chargeable to capital gains tax. However, HMRC contend that a greater value attaches to the non-residential part and eventually it is agreed that the gain attributable to the part used for the business is £250,000. PPR is available in relation to the remaining gain of £350,000.

Relief is only restricted where part of the property is used exclusively for business purposes. Where a small business is run from a room in the home, ensuring that the room is also used for private purposes will preserve relief. For example, a room used as an office in the day could be used in the evenings for the children to do their homework. However, there must be some actual private use – simply leaving private possessions in the room will not be sufficient.

29.5.2. Restriction 2 – Change Of Use

A residence may be altered or extended over time and its use may change frequently. Provision is made (in TCGA 1992, s 224(2)) to ensure that where the use of the property changes, the amount of the gain qualifying for PPR is adjusted in a manner which is 'just and reasonable'.

The provisions are wide ranging in their application; they bite where there is a change in what is occupied as a person's residence as a result of the reconstruction or conversion of a building or for another reason, and there is a change in the part that is used for a trade, business, profession or vocation or for any other purposes. The adjustment to the relief will again depend on the facts in each case. However, the adjustment should reflect the extent to which, and the length of time over which, each part of the dwelling house has been used as its owner's only or main residence. Relief is allowed for the final 18 months of ownership for any part which at some time has been the owner's only or main residence.

It should be noted that this adjustment is only needed for periods where there is some residential use, but there are changes to the parts used for residential and non-residential purposes. If a property is used entirely as a main residence and is then used entirely for business purposes, relief is determined on a time-apportioned basis, with PPR relief being given for the period for which the property was the main residence or fell within the last 18 months of ownership. For sales after 5 April 2020, this final period exemption of 18 months is reduced to 9 months.

29.5.3. Restriction 3 – Development Gains

The final restriction imposed by TCGA 1992, s 224 is in relation to development gains. The aim of PPR relief is to enable a home owner to buy a property of a similar standard in a rising market. The relief is not intended to exempt speculative development gains from tax.

Relief is restricted (by s 224(3)) in circumstances in which a house is acquired wholly or partly for the purposes of realising a gain from disposal, or where there is subsequent expenditure on a property with a view to enhancing the property in order to make a gain. In the first case, no PPR relief is available. In the second case, no relief is given to the extent that the gain made relates to the enhancement expenditure incurred solely for the purposes of making such a gain.

It should be noted that the restriction is not imposed where a householder buys (say) a home in an up and coming area in the hope that it will increase in value. The legislation is intended to apply where a property is bought specifically to make a gain, for example where someone buys a rundown property, does it up in six months and sells it at a profit. In a situation such as this it is also necessary to consider whether the individual is trading. A person who is in business as a property developer will be trading and their profits on sale will be subject to income tax rather than the gain being charged to capital gains tax.

30. The 36, 18 And Now 9-Month Rule

In this section you will learn about a key CGT relief whose tax saving impact has diminished in recent years.

30.1.   The Old '36-month Rule'

Up until 5th April 2014, if a house has at some time been your **main residence**, the last three years of ownership are always treated as though you lived there (for the purposes of working out the number of PPR years in the capital gains tax calculation).

This is the case even if you didn't actually live there in those last three years.

30.2.   The New '18-month Rule'

From 6th April 2014 to 5th April 2020, the rule became the '18-month rule'. This means that if a property has at some time been your **main residence**, then the last 18 months are now only treated as though you lived there.

The case study below shows how this rule can be used to provide residence relief during this period.

> **Using the 18-Month Rule to Get Full Residence Relief**
>
> Joanne buys an apartment in London docklands in 2004 for £100,000.
>
> She lives in the apartment for twelve years before she decides to move in with her long-term boyfriend. She rents her apartment for 12 months and then sells it 6 months later.
>
> The apartment is sold in 2015 for £250,000.
>
> Joanne will have no CGT liability on the profit of £150,000 as she is able to claim full residence relief; that is, her entire 13 and a half years of ownership is exempt from CGT. This is because for 12 years the property was her PPR and therefore there is no CGT liability on this period of ownership.
>
> Also, she is able to claim the **18-month rule**, which means that the last 18 months of ownership i.e. when the property was let are also exempt from CGT.

30.3.   The Newer '9-month Rule'

From 6th April 2020, the rule has now changed to the '9-month rule'. This means that if a property has at some time been your **main residence**, then the last 9 months are now only treated as though you lived there.

31. Private Letting Relief

> If you sold a property before 6th April 2020, and still had a taxable capital gain after using the 18-month rule (reduced to 9 month from 6th April 2020), then it is possible that any tax liability can be eliminated by using the **private letting relief**.

HMRC state that the private letting relief can be used where

- you sell a dwelling house which is, or has been, your only or main residence, and

- part or all of it has at some time in your period of ownership been let as a residential accommodation.

The amount of private letting relief that can be claimed cannot be greater than £40,000, and it must be the lowest of the following three values:

- £40,000;

- the amount of private residence relief that has already been claimed;

- the amount of any chargeable gain that is made due to the letting; that is, this is the amount that is attributed to the increase in the property value during the period it was let.

The use of this relief is best illustrated via the following case study.

Private Letting Relief

Roger buys a three-bedroom semi-detached house in North Wales for £50,000 in 1990.

He lives in the house for two years and then decides to move to a bigger four-bedroom detached house. He rents out the three-bedroom house for the next five years.

In 1997 he sells the three-bedroom house for £120,000. This means that he has made a capital gain of £70,000.

5/7ths of the profit is exempt from CGT because he is able to claim partial residence relief (two years PPR and the 36-month rule).

This means that he is only liable to pay CGT on the remaining £20,000 of chargeable gain. However, Roger is also able to claim private letting relief, and the amount he can claim is the lowest of the following three values:

- £40,000;
- amount of private residence relief already claimed is £50,000;

- amount of any chargeable gain that is made due to the letting is £20,000 (assuming that property increased by £10,000 in each of the two years that the property was let).

This means that Roger is allowed to claim private letting relief of £20,000 as this is the lowest of the three values.

Therefore, the outstanding chargeable gain of £20,000 is cancelled out by this relief, which means that he has absolutely no CGT liability.

In other words, Roger has made a tax-free capital gain of £70,000 just by having lived in a property for two years!

31.1. The Abolishment Of Private Lettings Relief – April 6th 2020

For some already reeling from the restriction on mortgage interest tax relief and additional rates of stamp duty land tax, the government's proposed abolition of lettings relief, as well as a reduction in principal private residence (PPR) relief, was viewed as the final straw.

The taxpayers most affected by the changes will be those dubbed 'accidental landlords'. These are broadly individuals who have rented their properties out of necessity; for example, a contractor who has let out their home when a job required them to move abroad for a year; or a divorcee who has rented out a previously shared property after a separation. In these cases, any increase in the value of their home will most likely incur a greater capital gains tax (CGT) bill if the sale of the property takes place after 5 April 2020.

31.1.1. Restricted Relief

The reduction in lettings relief is the main reason for this increased tax bill. At present, lettings relief provides up to £40,000 of relief (£80,000 for a couple) to landlords who let out a property that is - or previously was - their main residence.

From April 2020, lettings relief will apply only where the owner is sharing occupancy of the home with a tenant. For some higher rate taxpayers, this additional tax charge of up to £11,200 changes the playing field considerably; those landlords who are interested in maintaining a tax-efficient investment strategy may wish to act sooner rather than later.

If a property has been let to tenants, the owner will have to pay CGT on their taxable gain after the sale is made. The tax liability will fluctuate depending on how long they lived in the property. Landlords are presently able to take advantage of PPR relief, meaning that they are not required to pay any CGT for the proportion of years in which their rental property was their main residence. The chargeable gain is therefore directly correlated to the number of years spent living within the property.

31.1.2. From Bad To Worse…

In addition to this, landlords are granted an extra exemption for the last 18 months of ownership, even if they did not actually reside at the property during this time. However, from April 2020 this exemption will be reduced to nine months. For less expensive homes, the effect of this is smaller when compared to the loss of lettings relief, but it will certainly affect those who have only recently begun to rent their property (i.e. under 18 months).

The combined loss of lettings relief and the reduction to PPR relief will be felt by many, to varying degrees. While it is difficult to represent the effect this will have in each individual case by way of example, we can compare a sale made in the present day to one made in the future.

Private letting Relief And Sale Of Former Private Residence

Selling Before 6th April 2020

A landlord makes a sale of a property which they had owned for 12 years; their total gain on the sale is £120,000 (Note: each individual has a tax-free capital gains allowance of £12,000, but for the purposes of this example we're assuming this has already been utilised elsewhere).

Let's say the landlord had lived in the property for the first six years, only letting it out for the remaining years. As the home was their private residence for the first 50% of ownership, they would be eligible to take advantage of PPR relief. They are also able to claim PPR relief for the last 18 months of ownership. This subtracts a total of seven and a half years (62.5%) from their 12-year ownership, and as a result, they will not pay tax on £75,000 of the total gain. The remaining 37.5% (i.e. £45,000) of their total gain is not covered by PPR relief and so this would be the taxable gain.

Up until 5th April 2020, the seller is eligible to claim a further £40,000 of lettings relief on this. This has the effect of further reducing the taxable gain to a mere £5,000.

If the seller was a basic rate taxpayer, they would pay CGT on residential property at a rate of 18%, leaving them with a CGT liability of only £900. For a higher-rate taxpayer, the CGT rate on residential property rises to 28% but still, their total gain of £120,000 has accrued a mere £1,400 tax bill.

Selling From 6th April 2020 Onwards

From 6 April 2020, the same property transaction would incur an increased tax liability. The landlord would be able to claim PPR relief for the first six years of ownership but only an additional nine months, reduced from the eighteen previously. This subtracts a total of six years and nine months (56%) from their 12-year ownership and as a result, they will not pay tax on £67,500 of the total gain. The remaining 43.8% (i.e. £52,500) of the taxable gain is not covered by PPR relief and so this would be the new taxable gain.

In this example, it makes a marginal difference when compared to the loss of

---

£40,000 in claimable lettings relief. As there would be no further tax relief to take advantage of, our landlord would be left with this chargeable gain of £52,560, rather than the £5,000 in the present-day example. Our higher-rate income taxpayer, paying CGT at 28% on the full amount of the gain, would see their tax bill rise to a total of £14,700; a 1050% increase.

Of course, the benefits of lettings relief are felt most strongly on smaller gains around the £40,000 mark (£80,000 for couples). Assuming no upgrades or refurbishments are made to the property, a total gain of £120,000 would usually only be accrued through long-term ownership. Therefore, it will be newer landlords who will end up paying more tax than anticipated as a result of the removal of lettings relief.

As the abolition of lettings relief does not affect landlords who have never lived in their property or owner-occupiers, the effects of the changes to lettings relief and PPR relief will be felt by newer landlords and those who may have had no choice but to rent their homes in order to keep them.

32. Increasing Property Value And Avoiding Tax

In this section you will become familiar with a tax relief that allows you to claim capital gains relief on the first 12 months of property ownership.

You will also learn how property developers are taking advantage of this relief to grow property portfolios without incurring a CGT liability.

32.1. No CGT On The First 12 Months Of Ownership

More and more investors are increasingly facing a situation where they purchase a property but are unable to occupy it immediately due to a variety of legitimate reasons.

- You are having the property built, or

- You are altering or re-decorating the property, or

- You remain in your old home whilst you are selling it.

If you are unable to move into the property immediately after you have purchased it, then it is possible to claim 12 months' relief. What this means is that the first 12 months of ownership will still be exempt from any capital gains tax. This is regardless of whether you currently have another property that is your main residence.

However, in order to claim this relief, you *must* occupy the property within 12 months of the purchase. And a condition of the relief is that after moving in you stay in the property long enough for it to become your qualifying main residence.

First 12 Months of Ownership

Asif lives with his family in a two-bedroom terraced house.

In January 1998 he buys a run-down three-bedroom semi-detached property that requires a significant amount of development and modernisation. The property is purchased for £70,000.

The development and modernisation work starts in February 1998 and is completed 10 months later, in December 1998. The total cost of the project is £20,000.

Before he moves into the property with his family, Asif has the property valued at £120,000. This means that the property has appreciated by £30,000 (i.e., 120,000 − (£70,000 + £20,000)).

There will be no tax liability on the gain of £30,000. This is because for the purposes of working out the number of PPR years in the capital gains tax calculation the first year can be treated as though Asif and his family actually lived in the property.

32.2. Using The Rule To Grow A Portfolio Without Paying CGT

Using the **first 12 months of ownership rule** is quite an effective property tax–saving strategy for builders and property developers. This is because they are able to build/develop a property whilst living out of another property. When the new property is ready, they are able to rent out or sell the existing property before moving into the new property.

Exploiting the First 12 Months of Ownership Rule

Alex is a property builder by trade who lives out of his two-bedroom apartment.

He decides to build his own three-bedroom detached house. The house is completed within 12 months of purchasing the land, so he decides to rent out the apartment and move into the new three-bedroom house.

18 months later, he sells the apartment and buys another piece of land, and this time he builds a four-bedroom property. Again, it is built and occupied within 12 months, and again he rents out the existing property.

Alex carries on with this cycle of selling his let property and buying land in order to build a bigger house, which he occupies within 12 months.

On the sale of each property Alex will have no CGT liability. This is because

- the first 12 months will be exempt from tax;
- the time he lives in the property will also be exempt from CGT;
- and the last 18 months of ownership will also be exempt from CGT.
  For sales after 5 April 2020, this final period exemption of 18 months is reduced to 9 months.

The tax strategy demonstrated in the above case study illustrates how you can quite effectively grow a portfolio and avoid having a CGT liability. However, as demonstrated in the case study, you would need to be prepared to relocate every four to five years to take advantage of the tax-free gain.

This strategy can be used equally well for property developers who buy run-down properties and then move into them before moving onto the next project.

Be wary of HMRC!
By using the above strategy, Alex will be able to avoid paying CGT as he is genuinely living in a property for a decent period of time. If you try to adopt such a strategy on a smaller timescale, i.e., where you move more frequently, then HMRC may well challenge your motive, and you may be liable to pay income tax on the sale of your properties—**so be warned**!

33. Nominating Residence To Avoid CGT

In this section you will understand how people with more than one family home can limit or even avoid CGT on the sale of their second homes.

33.1.   Having More Than One Family Home

If you have purchased a second home over the past years, it is extremely likely that you will face a considerable CGT liability when you decide to sell it.

A common scenario for having a second home is if you live in a city/town that is close to your place of work but also own a property where you go to spend your vacations, e.g., on the southeast coast of England.

If you are able to own multiple homes, then you may well save a considerable amount of tax by nominating your residence to HMRC.

33.2.   Nominating Your Residence to HMRC

If you decide to sell a property, consider nominating it as your main residence to save on tax.

In order to make a nomination you must:

a)   inform HMRC in writing which property is your main residence;
b)   make the nomination within two years after acquiring the second property.

> **REMEMBER:** A property cannot be nominated as your main residence if it is let out.

The following case study demonstrates how a potential CGT liability can be wiped out by nominating a different residence.

Switching Residence to Avoid CGT

Bill lives in a two-bedroom apartment in London and works as a stock broker in the heart of the city centre. He purchased his apartment in June 1995.

In June 1999 he also decides to buy a semi-detached three-bedroom house in Southampton that is just by the coast. He starts to spend most of his weekends there with his girlfriend.

In April 2001 Bill realises that his house in Southampton has significantly increased in value and that he will face a considerable CGT liability if he decides to sell.

He takes professional advice and is told to nominate his house in Southampton as his main residence.

He therefore notifies HMRC in writing that the house in Southampton is his 'nominated' main residence. This is done in June 2001 and means that the house is treated as his main residence from June 1999[4].

Bill decides to sell the house in June 2003 for a £150,000 profit and has no CGT liability. This is because

a) the house is exempt for the first two years because it has been nominated as his main residence;
b) the last two years are exempt due to the old 36-month rule

Once the house has been sold, Bill notifies HMRC that his London apartment is now his main residence from June 2001 (i.e., from two years ago). This means that when he sells his apartment in June 2005, 8/10ths of partial residence relief can be claimed.

This is determined as follows.

- Bill has owned the apartment for 10 years.

- Four years partial residence relief is due because between June 1995 and June 1999 it was his classed as his main residence.

- An additional four years' partial residence relief is due because between June 2001 and June 2005 it was again classed as his main residence.

This means that by switching and nominating his main residence, Bill has totally avoided any CGT liability on his three-bedroom house and also achieved a considerable reduction in the capital gain on his London apartment.

---

[4]A principle private residence election can be backdated to take effect at a date two years before the date of the election

34. Other Ways To Reduce Your CGT Bill

In this section you will learn how you can reduce your CGT liability even further by

- using your annual CGT allowance;
- offsetting previous capital losses;
- timing the sale of your property.

34.1. Using Your Annual CGT Allowance

Each individual has a capital gains tax allowance that can be claimed in the tax year. What this means is that if you have made a capital gain on the sale of an asset, then you can offset the CGT allowance for the tax year in which the asset was sold.

When making a sale with a capital gain, it is important to understand the following two key points:

- if the entire allowance has already been claimed in the tax year, then it cannot be claimed again in the same tax year;

- if part of the allowance has already been claimed in the tax year, then only the outstanding unclaimed amount can be claimed.

The CGT allowances for the current and previous tax years are detailed in the table below.

	Tax Year	
	2020-2021	**2019-2020**
CGT Allowance	£12,300	£12,000

The following case study helps to explain how the allowance can be used:

Claiming the Entire Personal CGT Allowance

Bill sells his investment property on 10th April 2016 and has a £12,300 capital gain.

The only tax allowance he is able to claim is his personal CGT allowance, which is £11,300 for 2017–2018, and to date, this has not been claimed.

This means that after this allowance has been deducted from his capital gain (i.e., £12,300 – £11,300) he is liable to pay tax on the remaining gain of £1,000.

If Bill sells another qualifying asset with a capital gain in the 2017–2018 tax year, then he is not able to use his personal CGT allowance again.

This is because the entire CGT allowance for that tax year has already been used.

Claiming Partial Personal CGT Allowance

Samantha sells her investment property on 10th April 2017 and has a £6,000 capital gain.

The only tax allowance she is able to claim is his personal CGT allowance, which is £11,300 for 2017–2018, and to date, this has not been claimed.

This means that she has no a CGT liability as the allowance of £11,300 is greater than her £6,000 gain. Furthermore, she still has £5,300 remaining from the allowance that can be used if she decides to sell another property or qualifying asset.

34.2. Capital Losses

If you have made losses on previous 'qualifying' assets, then you can register these losses with HMRC and offset these against any future capital gains.

Examples of 'qualifying' assets include

- property (e.g., you have a number of residential investment properties);
- shares in a company (e.g., you have shares in Lloyds Bank);
- units in a unit trust.

If you have made any losses, inform HMRC of the losses in the tax year in which they were incurred. For example, if you made a loss in a share-trading deal in May 2017, then register this with HMRC in the 2017–2018 tax return.

If you are unable to or you forget to register your losses, you can still claim these losses up to four years after the end of the tax year in which the loss occurred.

This is illustrated in the following case study.

Claiming Partial Personal CGT Allowance

Louise buys £20,000 of shares in Marconi at the height of the technology boom in May 2000. Unfortunately, the share price crumbles, and she ends up selling the shares 12 months later for a total value of £200.

This means that she has made a loss of £19,800.

She is unaware that she can register this loss with HMRC so that it can be offset against any future capital gain.

Had she known, she would have registered this loss in her 2001–2002 tax return.

After her misfortunes in the stock market, Louise decides to focus on property instead and buys an apartment in Birmingham in June 2001 for £120,000. She decides to sell it in June 2004 for £170,000. This gives her a capital gain of £50,000.

She takes tax advice and is told by her advisor that she is still able to register her losses with HMRC. In fact, as long as she registers the losses with HMRC by 5 April 2006, they can be offset against any future capital gain.

This means that she can reduce her taxable gain on the sale of the property by £19,800 immediately.

If you have made any losses on qualifying assets, then make sure that they are registered with HMRC!

34.3.   Buying And Selling Costs

What many property investors fail to realise is that if you have incurred costs when buying and selling your property, then these can also be offset when the property is sold.

Typical buying costs will include

- solicitors fees;
- surveyor costs;
- land registry fees;
- solicitor's indemnity insurance;
- local authority searches, etc.
- stamp duty land tax

Typical selling costs will include

- solicitors fees;
- estate agency fees;
- advertising costs;
- accountancy fees, etc.

34.4.   Selling At The Right Time Can Save You Tax!

The time when you decide to sell a property can have a significant bearing on how much tax you will save.

Before you sell your property, make sure you consider the following key pointer.

a) Beginning/end of tax year

If you expect to dispose of a number of capital assets in the same year, then try to sell them in different years to make use of your annual CGT allowance.

With just some simple tax planning you can phase the selling of assets to make sure that you always utilise your CGT allowance.

In particular, try to make sure you use up your annual CGT allowance before the end of the tax year. This is especially the case if you intend to sell multiple assets.

Timing the Sale of Your Property

John owns two buy-to-let properties, and in January 2018 he decides to sell them both so he can reinvest the money into a different area. John believes that he can achieve better returns by investing into an area of major regeneration.

He puts both properties on the market, and a sale is agreed on both of them.

John agrees with the vendors that the sale of one property will be completed in the 2017–2018 tax year so that he can use the CGT allowance of £11,300 for that year.

He also agrees that for the second property, the contracts will be exchanged in the second week of April 2018, again so that he can use the CGT allowance of £11,700 for the 2018 –2019 tax year.

If John had sold the properties in the same tax year, then he would only have been able to use the CGT allowance on the sale of one of the properties.

The Government is planning that as from April 2020 the payment window for gains on residential property will be 30 days from completion.

35. Using Property Partnerships To Cut Your CGT bill

In section 7 you saw how it was possible to set up property partnerships and how they could be effectively used to reduce your income tax liability.

In this section you will learn how property partnerships can also be used to minimise your capital gains tax liability.

35.1. Making Use Of Multiple CGT Allowances

One of the biggest tax benefits of a property partnership is that each person in the partnership can use his/her annual personal CGT allowance when the property is sold.

Using Property Partnerships to Save CGT (1)

Mr and Mrs Jamieson purchased a three-bedroom detached house in March 1999 for £175,000.

They decide to sell the property in May 2017 for £300,000.

They have not used the annual CGT allowance for the year, so they are able to each claim their annual allowance of £11,300.

It does not matter how many partners there are as each partner will be allowed to use his/her personal CGT allowance, as long as it has not been used up on the sale of another qualifying asset.

35.2. Save Tax By Transferring To Your Husband/Wife Or Civil Partner

In the previous section, it became evident that if you transfer/gift an asset, CGT may be due on any gain made at the time of transfer.

In this section you will become familiar with methods for transferring property between husband and wife to reduce tax.

DON'T FORGET: Property ownership can be transferred freely between husband and wife.

35.2.1. Transferring To Lower-Rate Taxpayer

In the following sections, references to 'higher rate taxpayers' and 'lower rate taxpayers' are only relevant to disposals before 6 April 2008 and after 22 June 2010 when the rate of capital gains tax is dependent on the amount of other income the taxpayer received in the tax year of disposal. As detailed in section 26.2, between 5 April 2008 and 22 June 2010 all capital gains were taxed at a flat rate of 18%, independent of the taxpayer's other income.

If your spouse is a lower-rate taxpayer, then consider moving a greater share of the property ownership into his/her name before the property is sold.

This is especially the case if you are a higher-rate taxpayer and your spouse has minimal income.

35.2.2. Transferring If Partner Has Registered Losses

In section 34.2 you learned that if you registered any capital losses, then you could offset any future capital gain on your property against these losses.

However, if your spouse has made losses in his/her sole name, then you can transfer part or the entire property into his/her name to offset the losses against the gain.

Transferring When a Spouse Has Registered Losses

Mr and Mrs Karim bought a three-bedroom detached house in 2001 for £150,000 on a buy-to-let basis. Both are higher-rate taxpayers.

Prior to the purchase, Mr Karim had actively and unsuccessfully traded on the stock market and had run up losses of £50,000. He had registered the losses with HMRC.

In May 2017 they decide to sell the property and invest in the northwest, where they feel they can achieve a better rental income and also higher capital growth.

They decide to sell the property, and it sells for £207,000, thus giving them a capital gain of £57,000.

Prior to the sale the property is moved into the sole name of Mr Karim. By doing this, they have both successfully avoided any CGT liability.

This is because:
  a) Mr Karim can offset the £50,000 of losses that he accumulated through his share dealings;
  b) the remaining amount of £7,000 is consumed by his personal CGT allowance for 2017-2018.

If Mr and Mrs Karim had continued to own the property as a 50:50 split, they would have had a higher tax liability. This is because Mrs Karim would have been liable to pay tax on £17,200 (after the personal CGT allowance for 2017-2018 of £11,300 has been deducted). (Mr Karim has his brought forward losses available to him, so he has no tax liability).

35.3. Transferring Strategies For Non-spouse And Non-Civil Partnerships

In this section you will become familiar with important considerations you need to make before transferring to a non-spouse.

35.3.1. Transferring In Stages

A good tax planning strategy for avoiding or minimising CGT is to transfer the property ownership in stages.

If you do this, then you can use your annual CGT allowance over a number of years to avoid CGT.

Transferring in Stages

Mr and Mrs Higginbottom purchased an investment property for £40,000 in 1998. They are both higher-rate taxpayers.

Their long-term intention is to give the property to their son to help him get onto the property ladder. At the time of purchase they appreciate that they may well have to pay CGT on the transfer at a later date if the property price has increased.

So, they decide to start transferring ownership by using up their annual CGT allowance. From 1999–2002 they transfer accumulated property capital gain on the property to their son using their combined annual CGT allowance.

By transferring the property in stages and using their annual CGT allowances, they have successfully avoided paying CGT on the property.

DON'T FORGET: Each individual is entitled to use the annual CGT allowance to legitimately reduce their CGT bill. Don't let the allowance go to waste, especially if you know to whom you will be transferring property ownership in the future.

35.4. Transferring At 'Arm's Length'

It is important to understand that whenever a property is transferred or sold to a 'connected person,' the estimated market value at the time of sale/transfer must be used when calculating the CGT liability, instead of the amount paid.

This is because transactions between such people are automatically treated as not being at arm's length.

Connected persons are defined as

- business partners;
- mother, father, or more remote ancestor;
- daughter, son, or more remote descendant;
- brothers and/or sisters;

- those who are regarded as close family by marriage, i.e., in-laws.

Sale Not at Arm's Length

Rebecca buys a property in 1980 for £75,000. Its market value in January 2003 is £350,000.

She decides to sell the property to her younger sister, Aleesha, at a significantly reduced price of £200,000.

It is clear that the transaction is between connected persons and therefore is treated as not having been made at arm's length.

Therefore Rebecca will be taxed as though she has received £350,000 from the sale of the property.

35.5. Putting Property Into Joint Names Before Sale

A capital gains tax (CGT) liability may arise on the sale of a property that has not been the owner's only or main residence throughout the whole period of ownership.

Putting the property into joint names with your spouse or civil partner or transferring a share to them prior to sale may save tax in some cases.

35.5.1. No Gain/No Loss Transfers

The tax legislation offers a number of breaks to married couples and those in a civil partnership. One of these is the ability to transfer assets between spouses and civil partners for CGT purposes at a value that gives rise to neither a gain nor a loss.

This can be particularly useful from a tax planning perspective, as it opens up the possibility of utilising unused annual exempt amounts and lower rate tax bands to reduce the gain on a sale of an asset. To take advantage of the ability to transfer assets at a value that gives rise to neither a gain nor a loss, the spouses or civil partners must be living together in the tax year in question.

The deemed disposal value is the value that gives rise to neither a gain nor a loss. The cost of the asset/share of the asset in the hands of the transferee spouse or civil partner is the same as the disposal value of the transferor.

35.5.2. Using The Annual Exempt Amount

Taxpayers, regardless of the rate at which they pay tax, are entitled to an annual exempt amount for CGT purposes. The annual exempt amount is set at £12,000 for 2019/20. If it is not used in the tax year, it is lost.

Thus, if a second home or investment property is owned solely by one spouse or civil partner and the other spouse or civil partner has not used their annual exemption for the tax year, transferring the property into joint names prior to sale can make use of the annual exempt amount to reduce or eliminate the CGT liability.

The following simple example illustrates the position.

Sale Of Holiday Cottage

Mr Smith has a holiday cottage, which he wishes to sell. The sale will realise a gain of £20,000.

Neither he nor his wife, Mrs Smith, have used up their annual exempt amount of £12,000. If the property remains in Mr Smith's sole name, he will realise a chargeable gain of £8,000, on which CGT will be payable.

However, if the property is transferred into joint names prior to the sale, they will each have a capital gain of £10,000. However, as this is less than the annual exempt amount, there is no CGT to pay.

35.5.3.   Reducing the rate at which tax is paid

Making use of the opportunity to transfer assets on a no gain/no loss basis can also be useful where one spouse or civil partner pays tax at a lower rate and has not used up all of their basic rate band. The share that is transferred can be tailored to secure the best possible relief.

This is illustrated in the following example.

Transfer Of Property Interest To Non-Earning Spouse

Mr and Mrs Jones have been married for a number of years and live together with their three children in the family home, which is their only or main residence. Mrs Jones has a seaside cottage that she purchased with money inherited from her grandmother in 2012 for £300,000, which she wants to sell. She agrees a sale price of £360,000.

Mrs Jones is a higher rate taxpayer. Mr Jones is taking a career break to look after the children and has no other income. Neither spouse has used up their annual exempt amount.

If the property remains solely in Mrs Jones' sole name prior to sale, she will realise a gain of £60,000, of which £12,000 will be covered by her annual exempt amount (2019-20), leaving a capital gain of £48,000 and a CGT bill of £13,440 (i.e. £48,000 @ 28%).

By transferring a share in the property to Mr Jones prior to sale, the couple can take advantage of his basic rate band and annual exempt amount. The best result is obtained by transferring an 80% share to Mr Jones. This will leave Mrs Jones with a chargeable gain of £12,000, which is covered by her annual exempt amount. Mr Jones will have a capital gain of £48,000, of which £12,000 will be covered by his annual exempt amount, leaving a chargeable gain of £36,000, on which tax of £6,480 will be payable (i.e. £36,000 @ 18%).

> This saves the couple £6,960 in tax.

35.5.4. Property Has Been A Main Residence

If the property has been a main residence at some point and has been let out, lettings relief in its current form will mitigate some or all of the gain attributable to the let period. However, has been reduced from 6 April 2020. From that date, lettings relief will only be available where the landlord is in shared occupancy with the tenant. Also, from 6 April 2020, the final period exemption is to be reduced from 18 months to nine months.

Where private residence relief is available, and possibly lettings relief, the decision as to whether to put a property into joint names may be more complex. For private residence relief to be available, the individual must have lived in the property as his or her main residence at some point. Where the sole owner ticks this box but his or her spouse or civil partner does not, putting the property in joint names may not always be the best option, as gaining access to a lower tax bracket or unused exempt amount may come at the price of a loss of lettings relief or main residence relief.

Sale Of Former Main Residence

Tim owned a flat prior to entering into a civil partnership with Neil, which he lived in as his main residence for three years, before buying a property with Neil. He lived in the property as his main residence for 36 months and let it out for 36 months. He expects to realise a gain on sale of £72,000.

Assuming the sale takes place before 6 April 2020, he will benefit from a final period exemption of 18 months and lettings relief.

The private residence relief is £54,000 (i.e. 54/72 x £72,000), and the gain attributable to letting is £18,000, which is covered by lettings relief. Thus, there is no CGT to pay, and so nothing to be gained by transferring a share in the property to Neil.

After 6 April 2020, the final period exemption is reduced to nine months and lettings relief is lost. Private residence relief is reduced to £45,000 (i.e. 45/72th), leaving a capital gain of £27,000. Assuming an annual exempt amount of £12,000, this will leave a chargeable gain of £15,000.

Neil will not benefit from private residence relief as the property was never his only or main home. Transferring a share of the property to Neil will only be worthwhile if this reduces the overall CGT bill.

Transferring a 16.67% share to Neil will give him a gain of £12,000, which is covered by his annual exemption. Tim's gain is reduced to £60,000 of which 45/72ths (i.e. £37,500) is covered by private residence relief. The remaining gain is £22,500, of which £12,000 is covered by the annual exempt amount, leaving a chargeable gain of £10,500.

Although the gain is reduced by transferring a share to Neil to use his annual exempt amount, the reduction in the capital gain is less than the £12,000 sheltered by Neil's exempt amount, as some of the private residence relief is lost.

35.5.5. Practical Tip

Putting a property in joint names prior to sale to take advantage of the no gain/no loss rule can be beneficial to use up annual exempt amounts and lower rate tax bands that may otherwise be wasted. However, where other reliefs are available, it is important to 'do the sums' as there may be trade-off. Also, the position after 6 April 2020 may be different to that before that date.

36. Advanced Strategies For Avoiding CGT

This section outlines a number of additional reliefs that are available, which can help to reduce the CGT liability further in certain scenarios.

Please Note: From April 2015 the rules applying when a non UK resident sells a UK residential property, and the rules for UK capital gains tax when he does so, have changed. See the chapter: **Essential Tax Advice for International Property Investors**.

36.1. How To Claim An Additional Three Years Of PPR

If you live in a property and then vacate it but return to live in the property again, you can claim up to three years' relief. This is known as the **three years' absence relief**.

It is not necessary for the property to have been rented out during the period that it was vacated.

However, for the three years' absence relief (sandwiched between periods of actual residence) it does matter if another property was your PPR during those three years, i.e. both properties cannot be your PPR at the same time.

Claiming Additional Three Years' Absence Relief

John buys a two-bedroom property in Manchester in 1985 for £45,000 and lives in it for 10 years.

He then rents a two-bedroom house in London in 1995. He decides to rent out the house in Manchester.

He moves back to Manchester in 1998 (after three years). For the period 1995-1998, John informs HMRC that the Manchester house was his elected main residence, since he was renting in London

When John moves back to Manchester he lives there for an additional three years and then sells the property in 2001 for £250,000.

This means that the property ownership can be summarised as follows:

- 1985 to 1995 he lived in the property
- 1995 to 1998 he rented the property
- 1998 to 2001 he returned to live in the property again

This means that John has no CGT liability when he sells the property.

This is because for thirteen years the property was his main residence. Also, he is able to claim the three years' absence relief when the property was rented out. Therefore, John has made a £205,000 tax-free capital profit!

36.2. Claiming PPR When Working Overseas

If you lived in a property and your employer required you to work overseas, then the period that you spent working overseas can also be claimed as residential relief. This relief can be claimed if you return to the same property and make it your **main residence again**. The time that you spent working overseas is irrelevant.

However, you can only claim this relief if no other residence qualifies for relief during the absence, i.e., you had no other nominated PPR.

Claiming PPR When Working Overseas

Alex buys a two-bedroom house in 1990 for £130,000.

He works as an IT consultant, and in 1992 he is asked to work on a three-year project in the United States. He jumps at the opportunity and decides to let his property whilst working overseas. His work permit is extended and he returns to live in the house in 1999, after seven years.

For the period 1992-1999, Alex informs HMRC that the two-bedroom house was his elected main residence.

In 2003 he is offered a permanent position in the United States, which he accepts, so he decides to sell his UK property. He has it valued at £300,000.

Alex will have no CGT liability because:

- between 1990 and 1992 he lived in the property, so there is no CGT liability;
- between 1992 and 1999 he could still claim residence relief as he was working outside the country;
- between 1999 and 2003 the property was again his main residence.

Even if Alex had bought a property in the United States in 1992, since he elected for the UK property to be his PPR, he could still claim relief on the UK property under both overseas employment relief and the last three years' ownership relief. If he had not elected to make the UK property his PPR, then he could not claim relief for the years 1992-1999.

36.3. Claiming PPR When Re-locating In The UK

If you live in a property and then your employer requires you to work elsewhere in the UK, then you can claim up to four years' relief. You must return to the property and make it your main residence again.

However, you can only claim this relief if no other residence qualifies for relief during the absence, i.e., you had no other nominated PPR.

Claiming PPR When Re-locating in the UK

John works as an IT consultant. As part of his employment contract, he works at different customer locations throughout the country.

He lives in North Wales, in a house he purchased in 1995 for £60,000. However, he is assigned to a long-term project in London in 1999.

His company provides him with rented accommodation in London, so he decides to live there for the duration of the project.

Because he will be vacating his house in North Wales, he decides to rent it out for an annual rental income of £5,000. He is liable to pay income tax on his rental profits.

John finishes his assignment in London and returns to his house in North Wales in January 2003. For the period 1999-2003, John informs HMRC that the two-bedroom house was his elected main residence.

After returning to North Wales he lives in his house for a year but then decides to move back to London on a more permanent basis.

His house is valued at £160,000 in February 2004. John will have no CGT liability because

- between 1995 and 1998 he lived in the property, so there is no CGT liability;
- between 1999 and 2003 the duties of UK employment required him to live elsewhere and there was no other property that was his PPR;
- from January 2003 to February 2004 he lived in the property, so there is no CGT liability.

36.4. CGT Implications Of Providing Property To Dependent Relatives

There is no principal private residence relief available to an owner if he doesn't live in the property but his relatives do.

However, if someone owned a property on 5 April 1988 that has been continuously occupied rent-free by a dependant relative since that date, the property is exempt from CGT when the owner disposes of it.

Dependant relative is defined as the owner's own or the owner's spouse's widowed mother or any other relative unable to look after themselves because of old age or infirmity. There is another possibly tax effective way of providing a home for a relative: by acquiring a property, putting it into trust, and allowing the relative to live in it rent-free for life. However, this is a simplification of the subject, and professional advice must be sought.

37. Understanding Inheritance Tax

Inheritance tax is becoming more and more of a 'tax bombshell.'

This is purely because property prices have increased so much over the past few years. If you do not plan for IHT now, then you could be passing on a huge tax liability as well as unwanted stress to your loved ones!

In this section you will become familiar with IHT and what you can do to minimise any future liability.

37.1.   What Is Inheritance Tax?

Inheritance tax is commonly referred to as a 'gift tax' or 'death tax.'

If at the time of your death you pass on part or the whole of your estate, then the inheritor could be liable to pay inheritance tax.

There is currently an IHT threshold level of £325,000 that has been effective since the 2009–2010 tax year. This nil rate band will be frozen, and will remain at £325,000 until the end of 2020/21. Anything above this amount is taxed at 40%, i.e., at the highest rate.

This means that if someone died after the start of the 2011-2102 tax year and the whole estate is valued at less than £325,000, the inheritor will have no inheritance tax to pay.

If the value of the estate is over this amount, then anything above the £325,000 will be taxed at 40%.

The March 2011 Budget announced that from April 2012, a reduced rate of IHT of 36% will be introduced where 10 per cent or more of the net estate is left to charity.

Please use the following link to view the IHT rates for previous years:

http://www.hmrc.gov.uk/rates/inheritance.htm

No IHT Liability

At the time of his death, John has an estate that is worth £240,000. His estate is made up of his house, which is worth £200,000, and the £40,000 cash in his savings account.

He gifts his entire estate to his son.

His son will have no IHT liability as it is below the threshold level.

Now, given the property price increases over the past few years, this threshold level seems to be *very low*.

If parents living in London, and the southeast in particular, were to pass away today, then it is highly likely that they would trigger an immediate tax liability on their loved ones.

This is because a very large number of properties in these areas are already valued at above the IHT threshold level!

The average property price in the United Kingdom in 2020 is predicted to be in excess of £330,000.

This means that more and more people are going to be subject to this tax liability in the future.

37.2.   One VERY Important Point To Note!

If you die tomorrow and leave the estate to your children, then any IHT liability is due immediately by them.

IHT Due at Time of Death

Death befalls Albert. When Albert died, he left everything to his son.

At her time of death, the estate is valued at £425,000. The son must pay £40,000 in taxes before he can take ownership of the estate.

This is because he is liable to pay tax at 40% on the £100,000 value of the estate that is above the £325,000 threshold level.

Now, in the above case study, if the estate was made up entirely from the value of the property, in which the son lived, then it may well be the case that the property will need to be sold in order to pay the tax liability!

Not only is there a significant tax burden, but there is also a huge inconvenience for the son.

37.3.   FOUR Simple Ways To Reduce Inheritance Tax

There is no IHT liability if a spouse inherits assets from their partner. This is regardless of the value of the inheritance.

Here are four common ways of reducing inheritance tax.

   a) Utilising the £325,000 threshold level
      If circumstances are such that your estate is not worth more than the current threshold level, then as mentioned earlier, there is no tax liability for the inheritor.

However, as we have seen earlier in this section, this scenario is becoming more and more unlikely!

b) Gifting to spouse
All gifts between husband and wife are exempt from tax as long as they are both domiciled in the UK.

This means that even if a husband has an estate valued at £10 million, then he can gift this to his wife.

It does not matter if it was gifted during his lifetime or at the time of his death; either way, his wife will incur no tax liability.

c) Gifting as soon as possible during your lifetime
During your lifetime, it can be tax beneficial to gift sooner rather than later. This is especially the case if you know who will inherit your estate.

If you gift during your lifetime, then your inheritor will be in possession of a potentially exempt transfer (PET).

A PET is a lifetime gift to an individual. If someone makes PETs amounting to any figure, then there is no lifetime IHT to pay, and if they survive for seven years after the last of those PETs, then there is no IHT to pay on death either.

> The longer you live, the less tax your inheritors will have to pay.

So, if you transfer a property or gift it away and survive for seven years, then the inheritor will have no IHT liability.

d) Trusts
You have already learned that husband and wife incur no IHT liability when gifting to each other.

However, if you want to gift to your children/relatives, then setting up a trust may be the best option.

Trusts can be used to hold properties as well as other appreciating assets such as stocks and shares.

Properties can be placed into trusts in a tax efficient manner, which can help to significantly reduce and even avoid capital gains or inheritance tax.

There are a number of different types of trusts that can be set up to make tax savings, and each have their own merits and are suitable for different scenarios.

It is strongly recommended if you are considering transferring to your children or other members of your family that you take tax advice from a tax expert.

37.4.   Don't Forget Your Capital Gains Liability

> Your capital gains tax liability is not eliminated if you decide to gift/transfer a property.

If you decide to gift/transfer a property, then you are still liable to pay capital gains tax on any profit that *you* have made.

Timing of the transfer is crucial, and if you are not careful when you gift/transfer, then you might be hit with a CGT bill and your inheritor hit with an IHT bill.

Double Tax Liability

Alicia bought an investment property in April 1990 for £125,000, and in June 2009, it is worth £485,000.

She decides to gift the property to her son in her lifetime.

However, she soon changes her mind when it becomes evident that if she gifts it in her lifetime, the gift will trigger a significant tax liability on the £360,000 capital gain.

Instead, she takes tax advice on how to best limit her liabilities.

37.5.   How To Avoid Inheritance Tax On Your Family Home

For most people, the family home is their most valuable asset. Unfortunately, it is also often the asset that admits them to what was once a very exclusive club – the Inheritance Tax club.

Inheritance Tax ("IHT") is charged on a person's "estate" (broadly, assets less liabilities) when they die. The first £325,000 is free of charge (the "nil rate band") and all the rest is charged at 40%.

Because the nil rate band has not kept pace with house prices, more and more people find themselves in line for what used to be a tax on the rich. Transfers between married couples (or civil partners) are exempt from IHT, so if the home is left to the surviving spouse there is no IHT cost on the first death, but when the survivor dies, the house may well have to be sold to pay the IHT.

Much ingenuity has therefore gone into schemes to avoid IHT on the family home, and these have been countered with much legislation.

There was a time when the ageing parent could simply "put the house in the children's names" and continue to live there – this has not been effective for many years, though sadly I still come across situations where people have thought it was, and get an unpleasant surprise when the parent dies and is still taxed on the value of the house.

The three biggest obstacles to IHT planning for the family home are:

- **"Reservation of benefit"** – If you give the house away, but carry on living there, you will be treated as if you still owned it for IHT purposes

- **"Life interests"** – If you do not own the property, but have the right to live there for the rest of your life, you are treated as if you owned it for IHT purposes

- **"Pre-owned Assets Tax"** – This is an annual charge to income tax on the "benefit" of using assets that you once owned in the past, or assets that you have never owned but which were bought by their owners with money that you gave them.

The tax on pre-owned assets began in 2005, but it catches arrangements made as long ago as 1986. Any future IHT planning might be similarly attacked with retrospective effect, so this is not a planning area for the faint-hearted!

Any IHT planning involving the family home needs expert advice, both to ensure that it works for tax purposes, and also that other vital factors are considered:

- Security for the person living in the house – some schemes rely on the generosity of the children in letting the parent occupy "their" house, but what happens if the children go bankrupt?

- The ability to move house in the future

- The potential problems if nursing home care becomes necessary (the rules on "deliberate deprivation" can deny local authority funding to those who have given assets away)

There are two sorts of planning to consider – lifetime planning, and "first death" planning.

37.5.1. Lifetime Planning

The scope here is very limited – but the following can be considered:

- **Give away the home, then pay a full market rent to live there** - but the rent will be taxable income for the new owners of the home

- **Give a share in the home to (say) a child, who then lives there with you and shares the running costs** – but if the child moves out, the value of their share will be included in your estate again

- **Give cash to the children, wait seven years, then sell the house and move into one they buy with the cash** – this works, but only if you have that kind of cash available in the first place

- **Mortgage the house, and invest the money in assets that do not attract IHT, such as shares in unlisted trading companies (perhaps the children run such a company?), or agricultural land which is let out** – after two years, the investments described will qualify for 100% relief from IHT, and the mortgage will reduce the value of the house for IHT purposes – but you have to pay the mortgage interest. I have seen this work, but only because the parent concerned wanted to invest in the children's company anyway.

37.5.2. "First Death" Planning

If you are a married couple (or a civil partnership), there is some opportunity to pass the home down to the children when the first of you dies – a dead person cannot "reserve a benefit".

The first essential step is to ensure that you own the home as "tenants in common" rather than as "joint tenants". This is because a joint tenant inherits the other joint tenant's share automatically on their death, whereas a tenant in common can leave their share to whomever they wish. If you are joint tenants, it is a simple legal procedure to convert to being tenants in common.

Some planning possibilities on the first death are:

- **Leave your share of the house to the children** – this is the "low-tech" form of planning, and crucially, it relies on the children's generosity in allowing the surviving partner to live there undisturbed (they cannot evict him/her, but they could put a tenant in or force a sale of the property), and on them not going bankrupt. If the survivor wants to sell up and move, there will be capital gains tax to pay on the sale of the house.

- **Leave your share of the house to a "discretionary trust" with your partner and your children as beneficiaries** – assuming that your half of the property is worth less than the "nil rate band" there is no IHT to pay, and when your partner dies they can leave their share to the children as well. If, however, your partner wants to move, there may be CGT to pay when the house is sold, and there is a danger that HMRC will say that your partner has a "life interest" in the other half of the house. A more sophisticated scheme is:

- **Leave a cash legacy equal to the "nil rate band" to a discretionary trust, and empower that trust to take an index-linked charge over the house instead of cash** – this needs careful drafting to ensure that your partner does not have a "life interest" as before, and it is essential that the trustees of the trust know how to manage things to avoid this problem. The main advantage of this arrangement is that if the survivor wants to move house, they can do so without any CGT being payable on the sale of the old property.

It may be possible to deal with this planning after the first death, by using a "deed of variation" within two years of the death. This effectively rewrites the will, providing that the beneficiaries agree. IHT planning is a complicated business, and it is **essential** to get proper professional help. I will leave you with two pieces of advice:

- Make a will
- If someone tells you they know a "simple" way to avoid IHT, they do not understand how IHT works!

37.6. Other IHT Exemptions

37.6.1. Completely Exempt

- Transfers between husband and wife; any transfers that take place between a husband and wife during lifetime and death are exempt from IHT.

- Gifts in consideration of marriage; it is possible for a parent to pay up to £5,000 to their child. The amounts that can be gifted by relatives and other friends are lower.

- Gifts to charities.

- Gifts for national purposes.

- Gifts to political parties.

37.6.2. Annual Exemptions

- It is possible to gift up to £3,000 in any tax year.

- Certain trusts are also exempt from IHT.

37.7. The Residence Nil Rate Band (RNRB)

For deaths on or after 6 April 2017 RNRB applies. This means that there will be an additional IHT nil rate band when the value of the deceased main residence passes to one or more direct descendants.

- For deaths in 2017/18: £100,000
- For deaths in 2018/19: £125,000
- For deaths in 2019/20: £150,000
- For deaths in 2020/21: £175,000

There is a tapered withdrawal of the band for estates valued at more than £2 million. Both husband and wife can claim their own RNRB, and one spouse can pass their unused RNRB to the other spouse. There are special rules when the individual has downsized from their main residence.

38. How To Better Manage Your Landlord Taxes

A message from Amer Siddiq, founder of:

www.landlordvision.co.uk

When I began investing in property, I naturally looked around for a software solution to help me to get better organised. I quickly realised that there was nothing suitable available and so I designed my own tool based on my personal experiences and input from other very experienced landlords.

My aim was to design an easy to use solution to overcome the five biggest property management challenges faced by landlords with growing portfolios:

- Getting better organised: cutting the time spent handling paperwork

- Staying legal: keeping track of safety certificates and legal documents

- Tenant management: accurately tracking tenant payments

- Income tax management: Knowing what is due and when

- Maintaining and growing a positive cashflow

Landlord Vision is the result – cloud based landlord software that is the only official solution recommended and endorsed by the National Residential Landlords Association (NRLA).

Features include:

1) **Rent and Tenancy Management** – A flexible solution for managing rents from different tenancies including single lets, multi-lets, agency lets and LHA lets, etc. Also now has the ability to collect rents from tenants via Direct Debiting facility.

2) **Calendar Alert/Reminder System** – A total solution whereby users will be able to see all their tasks in a calendar format, including rent arrears, tenancy end dates, certificate expiry dates and insurance renewal dates, etc.

3) **Expense Management** – A comprehensive expense management system whereby users will be able to record all their property related expenses and

track/report on them.

4) **Integrated Accounting Engine** – All income and expenses use best practice accounting principles, making it easy for accountants to prepare and advise landlords on their property accounts.

5) **Document Uploading** – The ability to upload and store images, documents, etc. into the software.

6) **Enhanced Property Manager** – Ability to store much more property related information such as logging of utility suppliers, property essential information, safety certificates, various insurance policies, etc.

7) **Enhanced Reporting** – See cashflow of a property/portfolio, including profit/loss, reports by expense categories and the net worth of a portfolio, etc.

www.landlordvision.co.uk

If you want property management software that runs on a desktop, then visit:

www.propertyportfoliosoftware.co.uk

39. A Final Reminder - The Golden Tax Rules

The challenge to you as a property investor will no doubt be how to grow a profitable portfolio. One of the easiest ways you can make money in property is to pay less tax.

39.1.1. Education...Education...Education

Whether you are starting out in property investing or are an experienced landlord with a sizeable portfolio, there is one thing that you should always do - educate yourself to make sure you are:

a) complying with the ever changing legal requirements

b) learning how to make your investments more profitable

c) making sure you keep up-to-date with tax changes that may affect your tax liability.

Although there is never a substitute for taking professional advice, you should keep yourself updated so that you can discuss these opportunities with your adviser at your next appointment.

39.1.2. Prevention Is Better Than Cure

There is a proverb 'prevention is better than cure' (believe it or not this was first said by the famous medieval philosopher Erasmus) and he probably was not thinking about tax when he said it, but it most certainly applies.

Planning for a tax situation you are likely to face is much better than trying to get out of a tax problem that you have unknowingly (or even knowingly) fallen into. It is certain that trying to get out of a tax problem will cost much more in specialist/consultancy fees and there is never a guarantee that you will get out of the problem.

Congratulations – You've now finished 'How To Reduce Landlord Taxes'

To learn even more ways on how to legitimately cut your property tax bills please visit: www.property-tax-portal.co.uk.

Lightning Source UK Ltd.
Milton Keynes UK
UKHW052312231020
372134UK00002B/6